WOMEN'S SPORT AND TRANSGENDER INCLUSION

First published in 2024
as part of the Sport & Society Book Imprint
doi: 10.18848/978-1-957792-73-6/CGP (Full Book)

Common Ground Research Networks
2001 South First St, Suite 201 L
University of Illinois Research Park
Champaign, IL
61820

Copyright © Helen E. Parker, Beth Hands and Elizabeth Rose 2024

All rights reserved. Apart from fair dealing for the purposes of study, research, criticism or review as permitted under the applicable copyright legislation, no part of this book may be reproduced by any process without written permission from the publisher.

Library of Congress Cataloging-in-Publication Data

Names: Parker, Helen E., author. | Hands, Beth, author. | Rose, Elizabeth, 1947- author.
Title: Women's Sport and Transgender Inclusion: The Counter Biological Argument / Helen E. Parker, Beth Hands, Elizabeth Rose.
Description: Champaign, IL: Common Ground Research Networks, 2024. | "First published in 2024 as part of the Sport and Society Book Imprint"--t.p. verso. | Includes bibliographical references. | Summary: "Following IOC guidance, many sports assented to a major change that uniquely affected women's sport. Athletes may now play in the category aligned to their self-declared gender, ignoring biological sex. Thus, a paradox for women's sport: while sport is a physical contest, biological females are now pitted against one special group of biological males, those who identify as women. Can inclusion co-exist with fairness, physical safety, and integrity in women's sport? Is erasure of female achievements and records acceptable? Are rewards, fame, affirmative programs, and sporting careers for natal females not important? Does female sport even cease to exist? This text presents the bio-physiological-sport science research that dismantles the myth of no performance advantage of transitioned transwomen athletes. This information is essential background to assist athletes, graduate students, sports administrators, the public, and LGBTQI+ communities to debate this hot button issue openly and respectfully"-- Provided by publisher.
Identifiers: LCCN 2023032926 (print) | LCCN 2023032927 (ebook) | ISBN 9781957792729 (paperback) | ISBN 9781957792736 (adobe pdf)
Subjects: LCSH: Sports for women--Social aspects. | Sex discrimination in sports. | Sex discrimination against women. | Transgender women. | Sports sciences--Research.
Classification: LCC GV709 .P224 2023 (print) | LCC GV709 (ebook) | DDC 306.4/830867--dc23/eng/20230912
LC record available at https://lccn.loc.gov/2023032926
LC ebook record available at https://lccn.loc.gov/2023032927

WOMEN'S SPORT AND TRANSGENDER INCLUSION

THE COUNTER BIOLOGICAL ARGUMENT

HELEN E PARKER, BETH HANDS
AND ELIZABETH ROSE

A link to access Appendix A Transgender Policies of Sporting Bodies, and Appendix B Transwomen Athletes in Women's Sport referred to in the book are provided as online resources at:
https://doi.org/10.18848/978-1-957792-73-6/CGP

SHARP IDEAS

The book series "Sharp Ideas in Sport" is aimed to advance existing contemporary discussions on sport and body culture through providing critical debates and challenging perspectives. The series is established with the ambition to create a hub for controversial, radical, and provocative views that challenge current insights into global sport. The concise pocket book format allows the general public to access our books but equally informs academic debate.

The rationale for the series stems from a trend in academia and wider society that controversial thoughts and arguments are often neglected in favor of popular or uncontentious views. Books, academic articles, and contributions to anthologies on sensitive topics that have merit but are socially or ideologically offensive are often suppressed. Such moral culture in scholarly work threatens the academic freedom that is supposed to perpetuate the status quo in our societies and therewith the future of our university institutions.

"Sharp Ideas in Sport" provides a forum that is detached from mainstream political and ideological viewpoints, and open for anyone who wants to confront mainstream as well as unconventional ideas based on reason and coherent arguments. A double-blinded peer-review process ensures the consistency of arguments, but authors are invited to argue against criticism if they believe the reviewers' verdicts are influenced by political or ideological views.

The book series thus aims to help readers to understand divisive issues in sport better through indiscriminate presentation of arguments of clearly defined sides, including those that do not match with the predominant narrative of being "correct". Our hope is that this will stimulate readers to sharpen their own critical thinking.

Verner Møller and Jörg Krieger

DEDICATION

This text is dedicated to all the girls and women who love their sport and wish to see it thrive and prosper. To all the mothers, daughters, granddaughters, sisters, aunties, nieces, and gal pals.

We acknowledge the pioneer women athletes who blazed the trail and broke down barriers to enable greater opportunities and participation by females of all ages. Women's sport now is rightly acclaimed, and female athletes' achievements lauded.

In this current era, we also commend the brave athletes, and allies of women's sport who are standing up to the infiltration of gender identity ideology into sports' participation policies. Their protests are based in biological science and the fact that male and female bodies are different. They are frustrated that with the incursion of transwomen athletes into their sport these biological facts have been ignored, compromising the rights of female athletes to fair and safe competition, and a level playing field. These female athletes and supporters have shunned the bullying, ostracism, and threats by advocates of gender ideology and have refused to accept transgender inclusion as a fait accompli.

We hope the biological evidence we present in this text will increase the number of people, both inside and outside sport, who understand that biology does matter when it comes to fair sport. This knowledge exposes the fallacy that gender identity is a fairer method of inclusion. We argued throughout this text that girls and women should never have been made to give up their right to sex-based categories to assuage the demands of male-bodied athletes to their division of sport, who believe they are female, and want entry to affirm their self-chosen identity.

There are several people who have made this textbook possible. Firstly, Jörg Krieger who first convinced us to expand on our original journal articles; secondly, Verner Møller who provided advice to steer our direction, as well as encouraging us to keep progressing; and thirdly, the anonymous reviewer who provided us with detailed feedback, and enabled us to set a clearer direction in the manuscript. Also, a special thanks to Helen Dyer who generously volunteered to edit our final manuscript. Her fresh eyes and insight were invaluable in the last stages.

Finally, we thank our ever-supportive husbands and families whose encouragement, and patience we never took for granted over the past several years that it has taken to complete the manuscript.

TABLE OF CONTENTS

Introduction .... *XIII*

1. The Paradox Exposed.. 1
2. Genetics, Sex and Gender.. 27
3. Females are Not Merely Males with Lower Testosterone 51
4. Unintended Consequences for Female Participation 73
5. Competing Priorities in Sport: Balancing Safety, Fairness and Inclusion 99
6. Competition Integrity and Inclusion..113
Conclusion. Closing the Paradox Argument 133

Glossary... *147*
Bibliography *155*

INTRODUCTION

Underpinning the right to play sport are the principles of self-determination, individual free choice, and freedom from harassment or discrimination, regardless of belief, culture, or economic circumstances. Over time, sport governing bodies have actioned these principles to expand opportunities in sport for particular groups, such as girls and women, children and youth, older people, and for those living with disabilities. Necessarily, for each of these examples, sports have regulated the competitor's eligibility in order to protect fair competition, to spread positive health and social wellbeing, and to recognize endeavors. Establishing sex-separated competitions could arguably be claimed as the most significant change in sport over the past century or so, by empowering females, opening their choices, and providing rewards previously prohibited to this 50 percent of the population. For those interested in a deeper analysis of this important change, we recommend the 2017 paper of lawyer Doriane Coleman, former elite athlete and member of USA Track and Field's Athlete's Advisory Committee on doping. It provides a wide-ranging examination of the significance of recognizing sex-based rights in sport, with particular emphasis on legal rights and the philosophy behind the hitherto protected female category.

In the recent half decade or so, momentum has built for sports to update their policies to explicitly include participation by members of the gender diverse community, particularly those who identify as transgender. Transgender people believe that they have been born in the wrong body, and transition to the persona of the opposite sex (sometimes neither i.e., non-binary) via social, medical, and/or legal means. Regarding sport, transgender people claim they should be permitted to play in the sex category of their believed gender identity either male or female, ignoring their birth or natal sex. This is a contentious change to the structure of sex-based categories. The debate on human rights to sport thus far has been framed around the psycho-social and wellness needs of transgender athletes, predicated on their need for affirmation through sport. One example of an argument supporting trans rights to sport is predicated on claims that one's gender identity is their sex is the paper by Ivy (2021). Our text takes a counter perspective to the 'transwomen are women' tenet by presenting factual biological and sport science evidence to counterbalance the rights arguments drawn from sociological studies. This evidence will bolster support for the status quo, that for fairness and safety to biological girls and women, competition must continue to be sex-based.

Transgender inclusion policies have been based on the ideology of gender identity. This ideology advocates that one has a gender that is internally perceived, akin to a gendered 'soul'. It is this internal soul which determines one's gendered self, not one's birth sex described as being 'assigned at birth'. Gender ideology holds that a spectrum of gender identities exists, with binary sex being an outmoded, fluid construct. To trans advocates one's self-perceived gender is one's true gender and if opposite to their birth sex, they are labelled 'trans' – a trans identifying natal male is described as a transwoman; a trans identifying natal female as a transman. This ideology claims that transwomen are women and that transmen are men. Those for whom gender identity aligns with their birth sex (the great majority of humans) are described as 'cis'. Consequently,

Introduction

gender identity ideology re-defines previously clear-cut, sex-based definitions of woman / man from 'adult human female / male' respectively to 'one who identifies as a woman or man'. Accordingly, under gender ideology it is one's gender identity rather than biological sex that must decide eligibility for either the women's or men's division.

We note at this juncture, that throughout this text, we will use the nouns transwoman and transman instead of trans woman or trans man. Our preferred spelling signifies that the noun 'transwoman' or 'transman' signifies a subtype of person who identifies as transgender. Our choice contrasts to the alternate spelling that uses the adjective 'trans' to qualify the noun 'woman' or 'man', which implies that trans is a variation of woman or variation of man. Our biological perspective does not admit this latter meaning, although this form of spelling is commonly used by many gender scholars.

Transgender advocates have lauded the updated sport inclusion policies as being progressive and fair, and an affirmation of the existence of gender non-conforming people and their human right to sport, including the choice of the category into which they compete Those who question these changes (we are among that group) point to serious, one-sided implications for women's sport arising from gender ideology which ignore the facts of biological sex. This text exposes how the disregard of fundamental, sex-based biology of athletes in favour of social gender identity creates unfair and unsafe competitions for females, which infringes their rights, and undermines the integrity of women's sport.

Chapter 1 explains the genesis of the current sport inclusion policies worldwide, and how the purported positive goal of greater inclusion and fairness for gender diverse and transgender athletes has led instead to a paradox – with greater inclusion and fairness to trans athletes, comes greater exclusion and unfairness for female athletes. We describe the pathway leading to the latest International Olympic Committee's (IOC) guidance to sports on transgender inclusion, released in late 2021. Despite existing biological evidence, which we explain in following chapters, this IOC guidance continues to promote gender identity as a central principle in sports. At the same time this fails to protect the women's category of sport from the incursion of female identifying males (transwomen) where male biology is the crucial factor.

We also review existing legal protections of sex-based frameworks embodied in various nations' human rights, civil rights or sex discrimination laws supposedly designed to provide positive discrimination and fairness for sex-based sports. Many of these laws have been amended to make gender identity a protected right alongside, or in place of 'sex'. We describe how such substitutions, and lack of clear distinction between the terms sex and gender, have created confusion around previous legal protections of girls' and women's sport.

Chapter 2 provides an in-depth description of sex and gender, particularly genetics and embryology, and the role that sex-aligned hormones have in human physical development. Crucially, we define terms such as sex, gender, sexual attraction, transgender and intersex. Each is a term with distinct meanings that if used incorrectly as synonyms, merely lead to confusion and misunderstanding in the debate about fair inclusion of transgender athletes in sport. The prevalence of gender dysphoria, the medical diagnosis assigned to transgender, and its treatment in transitioning are described. We expand on the biological advantages afforded by testosterone for males, especially post-puberty, and how gender transitioning hormone treatment does not reverse this physiological advantage.

In Chapter 3 we draw on biological, sport science and endocrinological evidence to detail the sex-aligned biological differences in physique, physiological capabilities, and sporting performance, and the unique challenges associated with female biology. These data show that within sports, male athletes have immutable physical and performance advantages over their female counterparts, and that testosterone-reducing, gender transitioning does not erase such physical advantages regardless of the passage of time. While research on athletes who identify as transgender is scarce, existing examples debunk the trans advocate claims to the right of transgender athletes to be treated as women, having no particular physical advantage over other women athletes. This evidence underpins our foundation argument, that biological facts should not be ignored but rather be given primary importance by policy makers in regulating competitor eligibility.

We emphasize that sport is a physical contest with rules of play establishing a fair contest among participants and in which the outcome is not pre-determined – the so-called 'level playing field' in sport. We argue that permitting transwomen athletes to compete in the female category upends the basic principle of fairness and the 'level playing field' since the superior physical capability of a male body pre-determines the outcome and undermines the integrity of the competition.

In Chapter 4 we introduce a number of potential, adverse consequences arising from the transgender paradox in women's sport and impacting female athletes. These consequences are rarely recognized or researched in the sporting literature. Whilst it is important to consider the consequences for grass roots female sport, most of the research which informs our position focuses on the elite competitive level. Research into effects of new inclusion policies on women's prospects in other sport industry roles such as team manager, coach, or administrator is rare, and advocacy for missed female opportunities in these areas remains silent. Although our discussion remains focused on the athlete, we do not dismiss the need for relevant debate among a wider range of stakeholders in the sport industry.

In Chapter 5, the argument shifts to describing how sports are struggling to balance three priorities central to competitions - how to balance the priority of inclusion against the priorities of fairness and of safety. We describe how the balance between these priorities is different among sports and that deciding the best way to include transgender athletes requires careful analysis. The IOC's 2021 guidance on trans inclusion also recognized the inherent differences in sports. It has ruled that going forward, sports' governing bodies would be responsible for their own inclusion regulations.

This chapter also addresses recent changes by some sport bodies that have taken on board biological evidence and now prohibit transwomen athletes in the female division. World Rugby was the exemplar in evidence-based policy, now followed by World Aquatics in late 2022, World Athletics in early 2023, and Cycling Time Trials UK in mid 2023. Grounded in biological and sport science evidence, these federations have stepped beyond present-day sociological arguments for inclusion based on identity to bolster the integrity of their sex-based categories in their sports. It is noteworthy that these organizations have proposed a meaningful pathway in sport for trans athletes at all levels of sport.

Also, we explain how, under current regulations prioritizing inclusion, there is a growing number of transwomen athletes entering female competitions. In this chapter, we counter the oft-stated argument that the extremely low prevalence of transgender individuals in the population means that their presence in sport makes no difference to women's opportunities. Yet, we reveal there are ever-increasing instances of transwomen athletes claiming unfair discrimination if not permitted to compete as a woman and making their mark in female sport. We have created Appendix B which lists such instances, catalogued by sport, to illustrate how the problem has escalated in recent years. Ironically, the successes of transwomen athletes have been mostly lauded by the media who promote them as role models and celebrities. However, similar attention has not been paid to the negative effect on the female athletes who are displaced from podium finishes, or whose records are broken, or who miss recognition or accolades. Where such attention has occurred, those protesting the unfairness of this, usually women athletes, are portrayed in a negative light.

Chapter 6 addresses possible solutions to the transgender paradox in female sport. We discuss both existing and potential examples from sports' participation policies that attempt to balance the competing priorities of fairness and safety with inclusion. Of the ten options canvassed only two are straightforward and based on biological reality.

Finally, we close the paradox argument by concluding that eligibility for the female category of sport must be based on biology, being for those of the female sex only. We conclude that gender identity, or reduced testosterone levels cannot deliver fair opportunities for girls and women in sport. We summarize the book by drawing out seven key messages or themes. The reader may even wish to start at the end and then delve into the other chapters for the supporting background content.

Our text is supported by two important appendices on the book's website. Appendix A is a comprehensive list of the current policies for transgender inclusion of international and national sport bodies organized alphabetically by sport. These policies are often changing but were up to date as of July 2023. Appendix B is a compilation of over 50 trans athletes and their achievements, drawn from the public domain. Understandably, this list is incomplete because the trans status of an athlete is a private matter and protected by current sport policies and privacy laws. Nevertheless, the list continues to grow as more transwomen athletes "come out", often as part of anti-discrimination litigation for the right to enter female competitions.

This text provides graduate students, sports administrators, and interested members of the general community with sound biological evidence and coherent arguments to defend existing sex-based sport categories and counter untenable arguments for inclusion put forward by trans advocates. Following the Conclusion is a full list of References and a Glossary of definitions of the terms used in this text.

The overturning of sex-based by gender-based sport categories is a controversial and live issue in the sporting world. We conclude that policymaking of sporting bodies has been negligent by restricting research to a sociological viewpoint, and human rights and gender ideology arguments, and not considering readily available biological evidence.

To merely shoehorn a newly defined type of athlete of the opposite sex into the existing sex-based category of female sport in the name of gender inclusion is no solution. The rights of women to their sex-defined sporting category in the name of fairness should not be forfeited so easily to appease the mental health of physical males who demand inclusion.

At the end of the day, administrators and sport governing bodies, athletes, and the community all want the same thing – fair sport, safe sport, authentic sport for all comers. Therefore, we have written this text with the following principles uppermost, and we encourage the reader to embrace them in continuing the debate.

Firstly, the issue of transgender rights in sport is a contentious social debate, weighed down by false claims and counterclaims, and is especially in denial of biological facts. Resolution of this debate demands *open dialogue* between those affected – especially female and transgender athletes. But the common response thus far has been to ignore the voices of female athletes and their concerns, and instead fall in behind the transgender athlete's wants and psychological support needs.

Many athletes or coaches who question the common sense of gender ideology in female sport have been required to undertake gender mediation counselling to be educated on "rights" and to update their supposed false, transphobic attitudes. However, education about transgender issues in sport cannot be solely one-way. Those campaigning for inclusion of transwomen in female sport must also be open to education about genetics, exercise science, and endocrinology research, and the adverse implications for the corresponding psychological needs and rights of female athletes to fair competition.

Secondly, *respectful discussion*. Trans advocates demand that sport must revolutionize to become progressive and lead societal change in gender identity. They assert that it is discriminatory and an infringement of a human right to deny trans athletes access to the category aligned with their chosen gender. Those hesitant of this change, who raise genuine questions, who look to the facts of biology, or question gender ideology are often labelled as promoters of hate speech, bigoted, transphobic, cis supremacists or TERFs (trans exclusionary radical feminists) by trans campaigners. Vilifying trans-hesitant commentators, female athletes, or gender critical academics for raising legitimate questions of concern shuts down dialogue. Conversely, demeaning transwomen athletes by denying they exist, and calling them cheats, freaks, or weirdos with suspect, sinister motives is equally disrespectful behavior.

Thirdly, regardless of one's social identity, in civil society each deserves to be *respected in their choice* of personhood and to live lives free from harassment and bigotry. We uphold that principle, and abhor hateful, bigoted speech designed to hurt people regardless of which side of an argument or debate they occupy. As it stands, transgender athletes are following the current rules of sporting bodies and so by the letter of the existing inclusion regulations are doing nothing wrong. However, policy makers have created the paradox for women's sport, producing a growing backlash in the community and in female sports against transwomen athletes. The target of dissent should be that policy, and those drafting it, rather than individual transgender athletes who are following the rules.

Our questioning of assumed fairness of transgender inclusion is not based on fear of gender diversity but aims to expose the one-way effect of biological advantage of male-bodied over female-bodied athletes. However, in the male division we point out that this one-sided impact also plays out, but in reverse. In many sports, male identifying female athletes (transmen) now are eligible to compete in the male division, yet despite hormonal assistance to masculinize their female physique in gender transition their increased strength and power never catches up to their male counterparts.

Tellingly, there is no reverse demand by trans campaigners or transmen athletes to compete against males. Unlike advocacy for transwomen athletes, there is no equivalent mantra that sport is essential to affirming transmen's male identity; there is no equivalent call for men's sport to re-organize to be more inclusive and fairer to this new category of man; and there is no equivalent concern that male athletes may miss team selections, face unfair or unsafe competition, or have reduced chance of podium finishes because of inclusion of transmen competitors. Biology dictates that transmen athletes will not match male athletes' physicality. Consequently, our discussion is centred around the paradox of transwomen in women's sport.

We are neither denying transgender access to sports and physical recreation, nor are we advocating banning trans people from sport. Sports participation should be part of their lives for social and health benefits as for all others. However, sport has always regulated the eligibility for competition in the interests of fairness and safety of athletes and to grow the industry. We believe that regulating eligibility for any competition cannot be characterized as unfair per se but as protective discrimination catering for the needs of the specific group. We contend that female athletes are one such group, and the female category of sport should be protected.

CHAPTER 1

The Paradox Exposed

Human Right to Sport for All

From its genesis in training hunting or fighting skills in men, modern sport is a socio-cultural endeavour in which individuals or teams test their physical skill in a contest to decide the winner according to formalised rules of fair play. Fair play is a defining concept that validates sport. It provides opportunity, lifts its citizens up, including women, empowers individuals through participation in physical activities, and promotes health and wellbeing, whether at the recreational or the elite level. The modern Olympics and international sports provide inspiration for athletes to strive to be the best and a source of national pride and international understanding. As a social institution, fair sport is deemed good for society.

Box 1.1 highlights statements of human rights principles in sport policy from the International Olympic Committee, and The International Charter of Physical Education, Physical Activity and Sport. Each invokes the concept that playing fair sport free from discrimination of any kind is a human right, underpinning individual health, safety, friendship and solidarity, and dignity. Such sentiments guide policies on participation, and ethics and governance of peak international and national sporting bodies. As Professor Doriane Lambert Coleman, who specializes in sex discrimination law and transgender rights, stated: "The Olympic movement itself seeks to contribute to building a peaceful and better world by educating young people through sport practiced in accordance with Olympism and its values … including respect for international conventions on protecting human rights …rejection of discrimination of any kind" (2017, p. 100). Expressing such universal rights strengthens the importance of sport, physical education, and physical activity in the lives of humans world-wide. The challenge for all sporting bodies is how to ensure the human right to sport is supported in a way that is fair, safe, and inclusive for all participants.

Box 1.1

The practice of physical education, physical activity and sport is a fundamental right for all…without discrimination on the basis of ethnicity, gender, sexual orientation, language, religion, political or other opinion, national or social origin, property or any other basis. **The International Charter of Physical Education, Physical Activity and Sport (2015) (Article 1).**

sport as a human right. Every individual must have the possibility of practising sport, without discrimination, of any kind and in the Olympic spirit, which requires mutual understanding with a spirit of friendship, solidarity, and fair play (Principle 4). **The International Olympic Committee (IOC) Charter 2020.**

Every person has the right to practise sport without discrimination and in a way that respects their health, safety, and dignity"(p.1). **IOC Framework on Fairness, Inclusion and Non-Discrimination on the Basis of Gender Identity and Sex Variations 2021.**

In this chapter we describe the evolution over the past several decades of so-called progressive participation policies of many international and national sporting bodies that recognize and explicitly promote the inclusion of gender diverse and transgender athletes in sport.

The Paradox Exposed

On the surface, this progressive change is welcome as previously marginalized people are welcomed into sport. Yet these inclusion policies have created a paradox around competing claims of fairness and competing rights in women's sport especially. Whereas sport has traditionally been organised around the biological sex categories of male and female, these recent inclusion policies endorse the concept of gender identity as being a fairer and better way to divide sports. Therefore we have the paradox - a proposition that appears sound in its reasoning (a gender identity position) but that leads to a logically unacceptable or self-contradictory conclusion (males compete against females).

Briefly, male-born athletes who identify as women (transwomen) now have the right to compete in the female division in sports, and female-born athletes identifying as men (transmen) may compete in male divisions. This change from hitherto single-sex sport is highly controversial, with female athletes and allies calling it an assault on their rights to fair and safe sport. Advocates of single sex female sport do not want to be forced to share their competition with male-bodied competitors for reasons of fairness and safety. On the other hand, those championing the rights of transgender athletes claim it is unfair to be excluded because they feel their perceived, gendered self is true in spite of their biological sex.

As described in the introduction, the reverse situation of transmen athletes playing in male sports rarely raises a murmur as these biological females who identify as men cannot match the physical prowess of their male-bodied counterparts.

Transgender Participation Guidelines in Sport

Over the past decade or so, concerted efforts by transgender advocates have demanded the human right to compete in sport according to one's self-declared gender identity. Activists boldly claim that transwomen are truly women (for example, Ivy, 2021), and that inclusion in the women's division is fair, it shows respect to one's social identity, and affirms one's existence. To quote transwoman Alex Drummond, a 57-year-old with male sex organs and a beard 'I am widening the bandwidth of how to be a woman'. Note, however while there is no universal acceptance of such a controversial tenet, many international and national sporting federations have responded positively to gender identity ideology and the calls for full inclusion in sport based on human rights.

Rule changes enabled both transwomen and transmen to compete in the division aligned with their self-identified gender regardless of their natal biology. While advocates have lauded this change as socially progressive, opponents label it as regressive to the rights of girls and women. The policies that re-defined participant eligibility to competition from previously sex-based to social-identity-based divisions in sport has created an existential paradox of competing rights – the rights of natal women to fair competition against other natal women (rights based on biological grouping) as opposed to the claimed rights of trans identifying males to compete in female sport (rights based on social gender identity grouping).

With the development of sport for women, fears of masculinization and male imposters into female sport surfaced. Authority over sex verification rested with the International Olympic Committee until recently, beginning with the sporadic physical checks of female anatomies of 'masculine-looking' track athletes in the early decades of the twentieth century by the IOC and International Association of Athletics Federations (IAAF, now called World Athletics).

Following resumption of sport post WWII, the IAAF abandoned sex testing in favour of a medical letter verifying the sex of all female track and field athletes. However, to deter document fraudsters compulsory 'naked parades' were re-instituted by the IAAF in the mid-60s, followed by a buccal smear test to detect the Y (male) chromosome. By the 1968 Summer Olympics, all female athletes submitted to the Barr test, a blood test to identify the presence of the inactive X-chromosome present only in females. Unfortunately, this procedure discriminated unfairly by banning a small subgroup of natal females with androgen insensitivity syndrome who failed this test. The reliability of the Barr test was subsequently shown to also be affected by many factors in women such as age, pregnancy, the use of oral contraceptives, fluctuations in the menstrual cycle, and breast cancer (Sharma, 2018). Consequently, medical experts condemned Barr testing (and its later iteration, detecting the male SRY gene in samples), as invalid for sex determination with its unacceptable risks of false positive results. Compulsory genetic test protocols were abandoned by IAAF and IOC beyond 1999.

However, such tests identified female athletes with hyperandrogenism, with naturally higher levels of testosterone than typical women, sometimes overlapping into the lower level for males of 7.7 nmol/L or more (see Figure 2.1 in Chapter 2). These were biological female athletes with polycystic ovarian syndrome (PCOS). The other group were athletes with the rare genetic condition 5-Alpha reductase deficiency (5-ARD) differences in sexual development (DSD), previously labelled intersex. Athletes with 5-ARD DSD are biologically male with male gonads, but the enzyme deficiency means their male sex organs fail to develop as normal and may be externally absent.

They are born with female-like organs, a vulva and vagina. At birth these babies look female, many are registered as female, and raised as girls, and only came to know they are biologically male at puberty when the release of testosterone causes masculinized physiques and sexual maturity.

With enhanced physicality from endogenous testosterone, PCOS and 5-ARD DSD excel in sports requiring muscular strength and power. One notable example of XY 5-ARD is South African mid-distance runner Caster Semenya. Female Indian sprinter Dutee Chand has naturally higher testosterone in her body than typical also came under scrutiny of IAAF officials in 2013 (see Worley, 2014). Sport authorities deemed athletes with elevated natural testosterone levels to have an unfair advantage over their female peers, and consequently in order to compete regulated that their endogenous testosterone levels be no greater than 10 nmol/L. This IOC and IAAF regulation of female athletes with DSD to level the playing field became known as the 2003 Stockholm Consensus.

Schultz's (2019) appraisal of the IAAF testosterone regulations for women athletes with DSDs concluded that fairness in female athletics was de facto re-defined as being about testosterone level. We believe that this 're-definition' of fairness becomes highly pertinent to the current transgender paradox. With testosterone level now the objective marker of fairness, it created a sanctioned pathway for others meeting that criteria to be eligible to enter female events. Female athletes with DSD and transwomen athletes, people with completely different issues, became 'united' by one common factor, their testosterone levels. A new rationale was made for inclusion that since transwomen testosterone levels could be reduced to the same regulated level as for athletes with DSDs then they too must also be eligible to compete in female competition. Our text is not dealing with athletes with rare genetic conditions. It is focused on the latter, small group of biological males who identify as female.

Yes, other social and medical requirements were also stipulated in the trans inclusion policies at the beginning. However, one inconvenient fact has been set aside by trans rights advocates time and again. Regardless of recognition of a person's gender identity, manipulating hormones does not and cannot change their biological sex (more on this in Chapters 3 and 4). In all sport policies addressing transgender inclusion, serum testosterone level became the key, objective marker of a trans athlete's eligibility for women's sport.

What are these testosterone regulations governing transgender athletes in participation in sporting competitions?

IOC Transgender Guidelines

In 2003, the IOC Medical Commission convened an ad-hoc committee to review the position of transgender athletes in sport. What became known as the Stockholm Consensus Statement set out conditions under which individuals undergoing sex reassignment after puberty (now called gender identity transition) were eligible to participate in female or male competitions according to their new social identity. Three conditions were stipulated:

1. Genital surgery, including external genitalia changes and gonadectomy.
2. Legal recognition of their assigned sex had been conferred by the appropriate official authorities.
3. Hormonal therapy appropriate for the assigned sex had been administered in a verifiable manner and for a sufficient length of time to minimise gender-related advantages in sport competitions.

This Consensus document guided Olympic sports up until 2012, but updated views on human rights deemed such onerous requirements to unduly discriminate against trans athletes, and their right to inclusion in sport. An updated statement in 2015, the *IOC Consensus Meeting on Sex Reassignment and Hyperandrogenism* removed the requirement for genital surgery and set a specific benchmark for testosterone levels for transwomen athletes - total serum testosterone to be below 10nmol/L for at least 12 months prior to their first competition. Of importance, the 2015 Consensus also included two provisos for transgender inclusion:

1. The overriding sporting objective is and remains the guarantee of fair competition.
2. Restrictions on participation are appropriate to the extent that they are necessary and proportionate to the achievement of the objective of fairness.

As it came to pass, the intent of these provisos seems to have been disregarded, as guidelines for many sports explicitly spelled out how transwomen athletes were to be included in the female category.

Until 2020 or thereabouts, most international sports aligned with the IOC-generated guidelines.[1] Beginning with the IOC regulations, sports are ordered alphabetically. It shows a wide range of sporting types with transgender participation policies – individual sports, team sports, non-contact sports, net-divided sports, invasion-game sports, combative sports, track and field sports, aquatic sports, cycling sports, and water-event sports.

---

1. A comprehensive, yet constantly changing, list of these sports' guidelines can be found in Appendix A on this book's website. The link to access additional online resources is provided at: https://doi.org/10.18848/978-1-957792-73-6/CGP

Common in these regulations is that all sports require verification that the trans athlete has socially adopted the lifestyle of their self-declared gender over a sustained period prior to changing sport categories (ranging from 12 to 36 months), with some sports also requiring gender re-assignment surgery, along with civil and/or legal recognition of their changed gender. In common, the regulations across sports specify the testosterone level for transwomen athletes wanting to play in the female competition but do not set testosterone limits for transmen athletes playing in male competition. This is because the physical masculinizing effects of testosterone on a female body does not result in either physical abilities or a physique that matches their male counterparts.

Most sports, however, do caution transmen to obtain a medical Therapeutic Use Exemption before joining high-performance leagues, as exogenously administered testosterone is a banned performance-enhancing drug across sport. Most sports adopted the 10nmol/L limit for transwomen though others such as World Athletics in 2019 and Cycling New Zealand in 2020 recommended a lower limit of 5nmol/L, and yet others such as World Aquatics, World Athletics and UCI (International Cycling in 2022-23 specifying 2.5nmol/L. To meet these various testosterone levels, transwomen athletes undergo testosterone suppression therapy, often supplemented by cross-hormone treatment (estradiol or similar) to feminize their male appearance.

Ahead of the postponed 2020 Tokyo Summer Olympics the IOC pronounced its 2015 guidelines governing transgender participation were no longer 'fit for purpose' and ultimately, in November 2021 published its *Framework on Fairness, Inclusion and Non-Discrimination on the Basis of Gender Identity and Sex Variations*. This new approach was to be implemented post the 2022 Beijing Winter Games. Framed around human rights to sport, the guidelines reiterated that all should be able to participate safely and without prejudice.

In contrast to its previous guidance, which specified catch-all requirements of testosterone levels and exclusion criteria in detail, this latest version merely set out ten principles. The principles are 1. Inclusion, 2. Prevention of harm, 3. Non-discrimination, 4. Fairness, 5. No presumption of advantage, 6. Evidence-based approach, 7. Primacy of health and bodily autonomy, 8. Stakeholder-centred approach, 9. Right to privacy, and 10. Periodic reviews. These principles were to guide sporting bodies to create or revise transgender inclusion policies relevant to their sporting needs, or types of competitions. This 2021 IOC framework handed back the responsibility to deliver transgender policy to each sport's governing body. It now took a back seat role by emphasizing that it had neither regulatory nor oversight roles over any sporting body, and therefore it could and should only set principles.

World Aquatics in 2022 and World Athletics in 2023 released revised policies under this framework. Of concern to many interested in consistent governance in sport is that there is no longer a common rule on transgender participation in the women's divisions either across sports or across nations. Conflicts have arisen between inclusion policies at the international federation level and the national sporting bodies in the one sport.

A case in point is the 2020 World Rugby policy banning transwomen from women's rugby on safety grounds, yet Rugby Australia's policy released later that same year permitted participation. As national bodies necessarily work within diverse legal, cultural, and political systems, varied approaches would be expected. One could speculate that policy distortions could arise when political imperatives of national pride, or commercial motives to 'win at any cost', or cultural-legal traditions intrude on a universal sport policy.

Another example occurred between 2018 and 2020, when a transwoman weightlifter was selected to represent New Zealand in its Commonwealth Games, Pacific Games, World Cup and Olympic teams. Some competing nations were caught off guard by this development, with differing views about fairness for women. The IOC is yet to address how it will resolve such conflicts, other than maintaining that each sporting code's international federation holds sway for Olympic competitions.

Several aspects of the latest framework have been widely criticized by researchers such as sport scientist and World Rugby consultant Ross Tucker, philosopher Jon Pike and developmental biologist Emma Hilton. At the heart of these criticisms is the view (with which we concur) of the incongruous focus on gender identity over biology in modern sport policy. Sport scientists conversant with the gender policy debate are incredulous that the IOC framework has disregarded already existing sport science research demonstrating that in almost every sport the biological attributes of male athletes as a group affords robust, sex-based performance advantages over female athletes. We review this research in Chapter 4. Evidence of male performance advantage beyond childhood is consistent and detrimental to a level playing field for female athletes if their division is opened to biological males.

For example, Principle 5 declares that sports make "no presumption of advantage", yet it also emphasizes that no participant should have an unfair or disproportionate competitive advantage without defining what 'disproportionate' could mean. We question how it is possible to objectively decide whether a performance advantage of one athlete compared to their competitors is only small, moderate, or disproportionately large, and in what circumstances. The line between fairness and unfairness becomes 'elastic' - when is an advantage too large?

Additionally, Principle 6.1 states that *until proven otherwise* the "no presumption of advantage" of Principle 5 must stand. This means that a transgender athlete must be permitted to compete until evidence of advantage in the specific event proves otherwise, notwithstanding the conundrum of defining 'unfair advantage'. Critics point out that this approach oddly reverses the burden of proof for determining fairness. Principal 6 requires the party upon whom a change is imposed (female athlete) now must prove its unfairness rather than the party who is imposing the change (transwoman athlete) having to first prove that there is at least 'no disproportionate advantage'.

Moreover, to prove such unfairness and before a trans athlete may be excluded, sports must now conduct case-by-case research to show what detriment arises from including specific trans competitors. Critics of this principle are sceptical that sporting federations are even equipped to undertake such research. To date, sports federations have not prioritized a research role, nor does the necessary scientific expertise exist within federations, and financial resources have rarely been dedicated to any research, and if so, are minimal.

A statement by Ross Tucker, at the time of the release of the 2021 IOC framework highlights the improbability of credible research being generated as required under the framework:

> …it [2021 IOC Framework] asks sport to compare a case to a typical group, where we know there is overlap, and to somehow prove the impossible, and assess when advantage becomes unfair. Passing it to sports to handle individually is actually right and makes sense, conceptually. [But] the problem is that the guidance provided in this handover [of sports making separate decisions on their own evidence] is unscientific, and is rather a political "nudge" (or shove), and the sports aren't resourced enough to do it well anyway (Tucker, 2021).

Finally, Principle 7 supports the human right of athletes to their health and bodily autonomy, stating that sport policies should no longer require an athlete to undergo any medically unnecessary treatment, including gender surgery or hormonal adjustment in the name of sport. In a controversial departure to the 2015 guidance, this principle declares that one's gender identity alone is a sufficient criterion for competing in female sports, thereby meaning that trans identifying male athletes may compete in a female division without physical or hormonal alteration.

Under this gender identity regime, transwomen athletes are also claiming the right to sex-protected spaces such as female bathrooms and locker rooms, whereby athletic attire is the only feature in common with their female competitors. For those critical of gender ideology, it is difficult to imagine how such a stance meets either the principle of fairness for girls and women in sport or safeguarding them from male imposters.

Regardless of such criticisms, the 2021 IOC framework has created new challenges for international and national sports governing bodies to update their gender inclusion policies but not at the expense of fairness and safety of their female competitors. For example, in 2022 World Aquatics and British Triathlon, and in 2023 Britain's Cycling Time Trials opted for creating an Open competition division, either as a third separate category for all comers, or as a renamed male category, which quarantined the female division to those born female beyond the age of twelve. In March 2022, Rugby Football Union for England (RFU) declared women's rugby is solely for those born female based on safety grounds. In March 2023, World Athletics re-affirmed its sex-based male and female sport divisions from puberty onwards, referring to inherent unfairness for females caused by immutable physical advantages from testosterone in male athletes. Therefore, transwomen athletes who wish to compete in the female division must not have experienced any part of puberty after the age of 12 years, and continuously maintain a testosterone level below 2.5 nmol/L from puberty.

These federations have embraced biological science evidence to ensure fairness and/or safety within their women's division. Around the same period, other federations opted for lowering testosterone levels for transwomen athletes in their regulations. For example, World Rowing reduced transwomen testosterone levels from 10 nmol/L to 5nmol/L for at least 24 months. International Cycling (UCI) reduced testosterone level to 2.5 nmol/L for at least 24 months.

Despite this, other federations, such as Biathlon Canada (BC) in September 2022 announced an inclusion policy that is fully consistent with the IOC 2021 framework. It enabled all participants to access programs and facilities in which they 'feel comfortable and safe' at both recreational and competitive levels below international events; there is no requirement for medical transition procedures such as hormonal therapy or surgery; and no requirement for any individual to disclose their gender identity or history to BC at any point.

Some sporting bodies distinguish between pre- and post-pubescent athletes. In most cases, for community or recreational sport the policies do not restrict the participation of transwomen of any age or hormonal status. For these forms of sport many governing bodies merely state goals aspiring to greater inclusion and non-discrimination. Regulations at the elite or representative level are more prescriptive. These goals are neither amenable to implementation nor readily compared with other sports as a measure of progressive change.

In January 2022, the National Collegiate Athletic Association (NCAA, North America) policy placed the onus on each sporting body to develop their own policy regarding transgender participation, and either align with their National or International body, or follow IOC guidelines. The testosterone limit of 10 nmol/L remains. Yet, although USA Swimming did develop more stringent policies (of less than 5 nmol/L for at least 36 months) the NCAA overruled Swimming US rules and permitted the first openly transwoman swimmer Lia Thomas to compete in the female college events for the remainder of that current year for the University of Pennsylvania. Thomas previously competed on the male team, transitioning during 2019. In the 2019 year, at the same meet as Thomas a transman swimmer Iszac Henig also competed.

At high school level, trans inclusion is based on declared identity and not subject to testosterone levels. In 2016 and 2018 Connecticut female adolescents were matched against transwomen teenagers Andraya Yearwood and Terri Miller. Between them over that two-year period, Yearwood and Miller won almost all the track titles in which they competed. Such examples created great controversy about the unfairness to female competitors and how to uphold the integrity of female records in the USA, against transwomen claiming the right to compete as females. This controversy is unresolved. The true incidence of transwomen competing in women's sport is unknown, yet the number appears to be growing, particularly in the cycling disciplines.[2]

While sport regulations guide the conduct of sport and are characterized as discriminatory (for sex, age, disability, weight classifications), they sit within the state or federal laws governing anti-discrimination. This next section addresses the legal basis of sport 'discrimination', specifically regarding provisions for discriminating on the basis of sex in legally protected female-only categories. We review how recent developments incorporating gender and gender identity into anti-discrimination laws have

---

2. Consult Appendix B on this book's website for numerous examples of transwomen athletes across many sports over the past decade or so. The link to access additional online resources is provided at: https://doi.org/10.18848/978-1-957792-73-6/CGP

created ambiguities for sex-based female rights. Gender-based sport participation policies are not laws unto themselves. They must abide with pre-existing national sex discrimination laws.

The Legal Basis of Sex-Based Discrimination in Sport

Anti-discrimination laws exist in many nations, particularly in liberal democracies, having evolved over the last five decades from equal opportunity, human rights, or civil rights movements. Addressing sex-based inequality and sex discrimination, the laws prohibit discriminatory practices of unequal opportunities, unequal benefits, or unequal rights between the sexes (male and female) in the institutions of society such as, education, justice, employment, and finance. The laws also recognized the need for special sex-based protections for females in areas where biological sex-differences created unfair opportunities. Sex-divided services and spaces designed to protect female opportunity, privacy, or safety are legal, with sport being one such institution.

The USA made early, legal strides to ensure equal sex-treatment in federally funded school and college sports via the 1972 Title IX Education Amendment Bill. This bill prohibited sex discrimination in any education program or activity receiving federal financial assistance. It mandated that female high school and college sports be allocated equal resources, funding, scholarships, coaching roles, and competition opportunities as male sports, to eliminate discrimination. Equal funding requirements under Title IX has resulted in a great expansion of sporting opportunities for high school girls and college women.

There have been amendments over the ensuing five decades to strengthen equality, however greater recognition of gender diversity and gender ideology has opened another debate. See Box 1.2 below for a summary of changes to Title IX over the past fifty years. A key change relevant to this examination of the transgender paradox occurred in February 2021 when the Biden Administration, in one of its first decrees, prohibited discrimination against transgender students in sports in schools and universities receiving federal funding. This executive order meant that funding and resources set aside for female athletes and programs under Title IX were to be shared with transgender youth and women (natal males) now legally competing in the female divisions.

Box 1.2
Title IX Education Amendment Bill:
Advancing female sporting opportunities?

Title IX is a 1972 Federal law that protects against sexual discrimination in education. It was introduced to require schools, colleges, and universities to provide equal access to sports for males and females and to create sex equity. This led to a significant increase in females competing in sports. The statute is, however, silent on whether discrimination is prohibited against a person's asserted gender, or in fact any mention of transgender students.

In May 2016, the Obama administration issued guidelines allowing transgender students access to toilets and sports that aligned with their gender identity rather than their biological sex. A student's gender identity was interpreted as their sex.

In 2017, the Trump administration rescinded these guidelines. Meanwhile many states had adopted their own laws, ranging from policies prohibiting transgender involvement to those permitting it.

In June 2021, the Biden administration made a new policy directive stating that discrimination based on gender identity would be treated as a violation of Title IX. Discrimination included preventing transwomen from participating in female sports or denying access to school toilets and locker rooms that matched their gender identity.

> The new policy directive stands against some US State-based proposals to bar transwomen athletes from competing in school sports beyond Grade 6 (12 years of age).
>
> As of September 2021, Alabama, Arizona, Arkansas, Florida, Idaho, Iowa, Mississippi, Montana, Oklahoma, South Dakota, Tennessee, Utah and West Virginia had already legislated protection of sex-based rather than gender-based sports. Legislators in more than 20 states have been considering such bans.

Education authorities across the USA are currently grappling with the consequences of this change, with legal challenges of discrimination and violation of rights from trans advocates to any state law prohibiting transwomen from participating in female sport. Equally, there are counter lawsuits on behalf of female athletes (in states which permit transgender participation in female sport) who argue that this is discrimination and violation of their rights to fair opportunity and benefit from female only sport. Such legal contests about competing rights to fairness in sport demonstrate that merely recognizing gender identity and decreeing that transwomen should be legally recognized as women is not universally accepted.

In the recent decades, other nations have introduced wider grounds for protection into their discrimination and civil rights laws. The international law which gives legitimacy to nations' sex discrimination laws is the United Nations Convention on the Elimination of All Forms of Discrimination Against Women. CEDAW's wording makes it very clear that it is talking about women as biological females, not persons born male who adopt female attributes socially or medically or have female legal status.

While CEDAW is centred on women's rights, contemporary views of human rights, contemporary gender and queer theory, and feminist scholarship appear to have permeated the original sex discrimination laws of the 1980s. For example, the United Kingdom Equality Act 1984 which originally recognized sex discrimination, and now includes sexual orientation, and gender reassignment within its section on competitive sport. Similarly, from 2013, amendments to Australia's federal Sex Discrimination Act 1984 (Cth) (SDA) added sexual orientation and gender identity alongside sex as protected attributes, at the same time removing pre-existing definitions of sex, man or woman.

No longer were the ordinary definitions of woman being an adult human female and man being an adult human male used. Gender identity was defined as 'the gender related identity, appearance or mannerisms or other gender related characteristics of a person (whether by way of medical intervention or not) with or without regard to the person's designated sex at birth' (Australian Human Rights Commission, 2019, 13).

Over time, the uniquely different concepts of gender identity and sex have become conflated, that is, they've become interchangeable. This has led to legal disputes about for whom a female- or male-only service is intended. Is it a service for one who identifies as a female or male; or is it for natal female or male persons. Under gender identity ideology, unscientific beliefs abound, such as that one changes sex in transitioning gender; a woman is anyone who identifies as a woman; a man is anyone who identifies as a man; a male can become pregnant and can breastfeed; and a girl or woman can have a penis. Essentially, the words "man" and "woman" have become virtually meaningless and according to gender critical commentators erase biological sex as a distinct characteristic of humans.

From such redefinitions, lawsuits arise asserting that since transwomen are truly women, transwomen have a legal right to access previously female-only spaces, services, or provisions, such as domestic violence refuges, hospital wards, female prisons, female toilets, and the right to play in the female category in sport. Gender identity has become the protected attribute and female-only services, spaces, or protections are now inclusive of anyone who identifies as female, including trans identifying men.

Common to sex discrimination acts in different countries however is an all-important, specific exemption for sport. Sport is permitted to exclude persons of one sex from participation in any sporting activity where the strength, stamina, and physique of competitors is relevant from puberty, defined as beyond the age of 12 years.

To quote from the Australian Human Rights Commission 2019 advice to sport: 'The objective of the (permanent) exemption [in the SDA, 1984 Section 42] is to restrict competitive sporting activity to people who can 'effectively compete' with each other'. This explicitly recognises that 'biological differences between men and women are relevant to competitive sporting activities. It can be understood as ensuring a 'level playing field'' (p. 24).

Therefore, while the discrimination laws explicitly permit lawful exclusion of male-bodied persons from female sport due to these unfair physical advantages, conflating gender identity with sex has resulted in assumptions that it is discriminatory to exclude transwomen under the Act.

In 2019, using the amended Australian sex discrimination law, the Australian Human Rights Commission (AHRC) and Sport Australia, using the transgender advocacy organization ACON (Aids Council of New South Wales) as consultants, jointly produced a transgender inclusion policy framework for sport.

This policy framework explicitly urged sports to take a progressive stance on recognizing gender diverse athletes' rights in competition, and to advocate inclusion, social justice, and human rights of all people. Inclusion in sport and sex-based categories was squarely based on prioritizing gender identity over biological sex. At the end of 2019 seven Australian sports bodies comprising the Coalition of Major Professional and Participation Sports (Australian Football League, Cricket Australia, Football Federation Australia, National Rugby League, Netball Australia, Rugby Australia, and Tennis Australia) plus Water Polo, Unisports together launched new participation policies for gender diverse athletes, setting out requirements by which gender identity became no barrier to inclusion in sex-based competitions. i.e., biological males identifying as females could compete against biological females.

A separate 52-page document providing advice to Australian sporting bodies on legal aspects of inclusion was released by Sport Australia and the Australian Human Rights Commission in 2019. While it aimed to provide clear-cut advice about illegalities of gender identity discrimination, its explanation of the permanent exemption under Section 42 for competitive sport within SDA, described above, was rather vague.

Advice on the meaning of a permanent exemption was first briefly stated on p. 24 and called the 'single-sex competition' exemption, and then described a second time on p. 36. As inclusion based on gender identity is uppermost in the document, the statements on permanent exemption for competitive sport is written in a guarded tone. It appears to caution sports not to rely on section 42 for exclusive single-sex female competitions as there are no legal definitions of the overriding characteristics of strength, stamina and physique, the very specific characteristics that may indeed disqualify inclusion of a female identifying male.

For those competitive sports that may believe they are exempted from discrimination under section 42, the AHRC advice sets out a listing of multiple steps, new roles and tasks that must be in place to demonstrate that a 'fair and robust decision-making process' is being followed. Our impression of the document, although well cited, is that in considering such advice sports administrators would shy away from common sense and favour the easier socially progressive pathway of inclusion. The advice implies that the pathway of protecting their female division from incursions by male bodied athletes is legally complex.

Interestingly, the words 'female', 'girl' and 'woman's' sport are rare in this document, yet 11 of 14 images illustrating the document are of female athletes. The great majority of case study examples of best practice are to explain how to include trans children or men identifying as female. It is clear to us, that this document is focusing on female sport to change. It promotes inclusion by only a single approach, that of re-defining a female by her gender identity and thereby inserting trans athletes in the female division.

A clear understanding is essential by sport administrators of such legal, permanent exemptions contained in sex discrimination laws and how they are designed to maintain a level playing field and protect females in sport. With the term 'sex', understood as a biological reality, disappearing from common usage and with gender identity taking priority in sport policies, the exclusion of a transwoman athlete from a female competition, in good faith based on strength, stamina or physique grounds is likely to be challenged legally. This is especially so with the guidance from Sport Australia consistent with the latest IOC guidelines - that transgender athletes should first be included, be dealt with on a case-by-case and confidential basis, and that specific research must inform an exclusion decision.

While privacy is an important matter, confidentiality may mean that precedents and decisions are opaque within as well as to other sports. A process that lacks transparency may be open to inconsistent judgments by sports administrators. We assert that the worst-case scenario for all stakeholders is that resolution of claims is sought through the courts – a costly, resource-sapping, socially damaging pathway for sport.

A legal analysis of biological sex within sport by Coleman, published in 2017, emphasised what should be well understood: that in her legal judgment, the concepts of sex and gender identity are very different under law. While she agreed that sex-segregation and sex discrimination should always be subject to rigorous challenge in any social institution, such as employment, education, or health services, she argued that 'where these (sex segregation [and discrimination]) are necessary to the attainment of valuable institutional goals, as in women's category of sport, they are lawful and should be affirmed' (p. 84). Her analysis is that sex discrimination law does not automatically grant benefits to transwomen, because in being biological males they are not eligible to be compensated for sex-disadvantages experienced by biological females; transwomen should be ineligible for affirmative action programs, equal opportunity initiatives, or quotas set aside for women.

She concludes that the law does permit biological males to simply 'read themselves into' the female category by claiming they identify as a female. Like other legal theorists she reasoned that while the right to play sport extends to all adults, such a right does not extend to a person who wants to compete in all or any sport category by choice. Specific eligibility criteria exist for age-restricted, youth or masters or disability categories for fairness. Therefore, Coleman reasons that the right to play sport does not in itself confer to all men, or indeed to any subset of men like transwomen, the right to compete in the biological women's category. This, she contends, is not discrimination per se but a protection in law for a valid, social reason, the advancement and empowerment of girls and women in sport. By this analysis, fair and meaningful physical competition is therefore delineated by sex-differentiated bodies or sporting categories, rather than by gender identity and feelings.

In substance, transgender guidelines for most sporting bodies underscore greater inclusion, wider diversity, and social recognition for a very small, marginalized group of participants. It seems that the guidelines make gender identity a priority over biological sex not only for organizing sport competition but also women's rewards. Indeed, the Australian Football League's Gender Diversity Policy (2020) for community women's football spells out this main concern: "considerations of social inclusion have greater priority than concerns that may exist with respect to competitive advantage in relation to the participation of gender diverse players" (p. 2).

Considering Coleman's (2017) article, one could rightly question 'why and to what end' is such a discriminatory stance taken against biological women, all in the name of inclusion. If sporting administrators are not concerned that female sport is now a category into which male-bodied athletes may now compete on their terms, then one could legitimately question what is the purpose of having a female category of sport at all?

Trans ideology asserts that transwomen are a true variation or type of woman rather than, in biological truth, being a particular subset of male. The use of the label 'trans woman' is indicative of this position (as explained in the introduction). Such assertions demand scrutiny considering the original intent of anti-discrimination law and its application to sport - to outlaw discrimination based on biological sex and to right structural inequities arising from one's biology, hence the female category.

There has been a growth in organizations strenuously lobbying for protection of sex-based rights, such as Save Women's Sport, Sex Matters, Save Our Sports, Let Women Speak, Standing for

Women UK. Such organizations fight against gender identity ideology that is pushing trans identifying males into previously female-only spaces, services, and programs. Advocates of women's rights in liberal democracies such as the UK in sportswoman Sharron Davies, author Helen Joyce, and academic Kathleen Stock; Australians, lawyer Katherine Deves, academic feminist philosopher Holly Lawford-Smith, and senator Claire Chandler; and USA sportswoman Martina Navratilova continue to fight for sex-based rights in sport. None of these individuals deny the existence of transgender people and their right to play sport in safe, fulfilling environments. Their views recognize the positive physical and mental benefits for people participating in sport. However, like these lobbyists our common perspective is that since sport is a test of physical prowess between competing athletes, biology does matter in sport.

While transgender athletes must have opportunities to play sport, an examination of biology and sport science demonstrates the female-to-male competition in most sports is neither fair nor safe. Even at community level sport, where financial rewards are not a consideration, enjoyment, physical safety, and fairness for females should be protected. For aspiring, high-performing, female athletes, these development pathways to elite levels and sporting careers should not be blocked by acceding to gender identity. These issues will be developed in the following chapters.

CHAPTER 2

Genetics, Sex and Gender

The genetics of sex and human sex differentiation is described in numerous biological textbooks. Contrary to gender identity theorists, the science of sex is not controversial. Although complex biological mechanisms are involved the formation of sex is well understood. There are many texts describing sex in human development and in health. The text by Wizeman and Pardue (2001) is recommended. In this chapter we introduce the biological facts behind sex differentiation from the embryo through to adulthood. This discussion identifies the sex-aligned hormonal drivers of development that change male and female children to sexually mature men and women. Terminology that is often misunderstood and used interchangeably is also clarified.

The Genesis of Sex

What does the label sex mean? It is an objective, specific, biological label based on a person's genetic make-up. Sex is aligned with distinct genetic, chromosomal, gonadal, hormonal, and phenotypical (appearance) characteristics. The typical human karyotype (chromosomal makeup) consists of 23 pairs of chromosomes, with biological sex expressed by protein differences on the 46th chromosome - 46 XX is designated female and 46 XY is designated male.

The human genetic code inherited from male and female gametes at fertilization determines the proteins, and structural growth of all tissues, organs and body structures as well as chemicals called hormones that guide the physiology of cell growth, cell regeneration and cell death throughout the lifespan. Genetic studies point to multiple, permeating differences in the basic cellular biochemistry of males and females that are a direct result of male-female genomic differences as well as the different hormones bathing all cells in the growing human from the early weeks of embryonic development and throughout life. The key to tissue development is the different effects of sex-specific hormones.

The most potent hormone affecting an embryo's sex biology is testosterone. This hormone is the androgenising (male-making) sex hormone initially released by undifferentiated gonadal ridge tissue in the sex-bipotential human embryo at around six weeks into development. Triggered by the SRY gene on the Y chromosome, the testes differentiate from bipotential gonad tissue and testosterone is released as well as from the adrenal cortex. In the absence of this burst of testosterone the gonadal tissue develops into ovaries which secrete the female hormone estrogen, although females continue to release extremely low levels from ovaries and the adrenal cortex throughout life.

Estrogen supports the development of the uterus and Fallopian tubes. Testosterone, secreted from testis tissue, supports the development of the testis, epididymis, vas deferens, prostate, and the seminal vesicle. These sex hormones produce the primary internal and external genitalia that identify human sex at birth. In these embryonic weeks, the effect of testosterone includes sculpting the body and brain in a male-typical direction, and at the same time suppressing female-typical development.

It is important to point out that the existence of several very rare genetic conditions that result in higher testosterone levels than normal in females such as polycystic ovarian syndrome (PCOS). In biological males, a genetic abnormality causing the condition 5-Alpha reductase deficiency (5-ARD). This enzyme results in failure to convert testosterone to its potent form deficiency of dihydrotestosterone (DHT), critical for normal sexual development and the in-utero formation of male external sex organs. In the absence of this form of testosterone, the male foetus continues to develop a female vulva and vagina, and at birth the ambiguity or absence of a penis and testis in 46XY 5-ARD individuals, leading to misidentification of the child as female. This condition was previously named intersex and is one of six differences in sex development (DSD). Further, Ainsworth (2018) describes how XY individuals with extra copies of the ovarian gene WNT_4 can develop atypical genitals and gonads, and a rudimentary uterus and Fallopian tubes. In contrast, female XX individuals who have a dysfunction in the key ovarian gene, $RSPO_1$, develop gonads with both ovarian and testicular tissue. The external genitalia may be completely normal anatomically but not always. Such genetic aberrations, of which about 25 genes are involved, exemplify the complex process of sex determination. The prevalence of DSDs varies depending on the definition used. The prevalence of individuals whose anatomical sex is not aligned with their chromosomal or gonadal sex may affect about 1 in 4500 people (Ainsworth, 2018) however with a broader definition that includes minor anatomical differences the prevalence rises to 1 in 100.

Elevated androgen levels in women are relatively common and particularly in female athletes, occurring on average to 1 in 5 women during her productive years of 8 to 45 years (Bermon, Garnier, Hirschberg et la., 2014). Female athletes with elevated testosterone via DSDs or PCOS are more prevalent in middle distance track events and are more likely to be African or south Asian heritage. The prevalence in elite female runners is cited as 7.1 per 1000, around

140 times greater than for the general female population (IAAF - World Athletics, 2018). At puberty those with DSD, often assigned female at birth although they are physiologically male, are positively affected by testosterone released from inherited male gonadal tissue resulting in masculinized physiques with stronger, more powerful musculature that are well suited to these power events. In women's sport, athletes with DSDs had testosterone regulations if they competed in events from 400m to the mile, including 400m, hurdles races, 800m, 1500m, one-mile races, and combined events over the same distances.

The case of Caster Semenya, the South African middle-distance runner and 800m world title holder is a controversial case in women's track events. Her naturally inherited elevated testosterone levels within the male range from DSD were deemed unfair in women's sport. To re-level the playing field for female middle-distance runners, the 2018 IAAF reinstated its testosterone levels for females that blood levels were not to exceed 5 nmol/L for the 6 months preceding competition, and over the duration of their competing career. Since March of 2023, World Athletics has further reduced the level to 2.5 nmol/L for a minimum of 6 months in order to compete in any international event. In the end, Semenya's appeals to the Court of Arbitration for Sport in 2019, and the Federal Supreme Court of Switzerland in 2020 were to no avail. But on 11 July 2023 an appeal to the European Court of Human Rights ruled that the Swiss legal system 'had not afforded Semenya sufficient institutional and procedural safeguards to allow her to have her complaints [of discrimination caused by unfair testosterone regulations] examined effectively' (Nakrani, 2023), and thereby her human rights were violated. Beyond 2019, rather than manipulate her testosterone level she tried the shorter 200m and long distance 5000m events (outside the IAAF testosterone restricted events). Semenya was not successful at these events and retired after the 2022 World Championships.

The reverse cases of males who inherit female gonadal tissue are far less likely to stand out in the athletic sphere, as female hormones do not have anabolic effects (growth stimuli) on body tissues and are likely to inhibit the full extent the male physical development during puberty. Athletes with these rare genetic variations of cross sex-hormones via DSD are not the focus of this book. We are concerned with transgender athletes (more on this below).

Some gender researchers, such as Claire Ainsworth (2018), assert that the existence of genetic irregularities mean there is no single criterion for determining maleness or femaleness and therefore the notion of sexual duality is an overly simplistic notion. However, most developmental biologists such as Emma Hilton describe rare genetic disorders as merely representing a unique biological subset of each sex group, rather than representing a spectrum of sex types. The argument is that such rare cases do not invalidate the dichotomy in sex classification in humans, much like people born with a congenital physical disability, such as no upper limbs, does not invalidate the concept that humans, as a species, have two arms.

In this book we will use the adjectives 'natal' as a biological designation of one's sex at birth, hence natal male, or natal female. We also employ the commonly understood definitions of woman/girl and man/boy as being those born biologically female or biologically male, respectively. Currently, dozens of labels are used to describe specific identity and expressions for those within the gender diverse LGBT+ community. We provide a glossary at the end of the book to assist with definitions for terms used in this book but there are dozens of descriptors on the gender 'spectrum'.

What is Gender?

In contrast to sex, gender is a more complex and evolving concept. Gender is the characterization or attribute aligned with the concept of being feminine or masculine, the norms, rules, values and expectations society places on the sexes. According to gender theory each has an internal sense of being female or male, almost like a 'gendered soul'. For some, their perceived gender may be not aligned to their birth sex. Gender identity is the subjective, malleable social construct relating to how one perceives their gender role, gender orientation, and gendered behaviours.

In Western societies, progressive views state that a person's gender identity is self-chosen and self-declared and may be fluid over time. In contrast to classifying people by the binary sex categories (male/female), gender is seen to be a spectrum of identities. The spectrum is anchored by female identity at one end to male identity at the other, with neither or a binary identity somewhere in the middle. Even though feminine and masculine anchor each end of a potential gender line, gender identity cannot answer who is more feminine or more masculine in their perceptions. On which part of the spectrum does one place a female who is living sometimes or always as a man, in comparison to a male who is sometimes or always living as a female? Where do you place a fluid identity (gender expression or identity alters over time) or a non-binary identity (a wide variety of different identities outside the gender binary) on this spectrum?

A spectrum requires the basic characteristic (in this case gender) to be ranked on a continuum from little to most, or lowest to highest by some measure. What is a smaller amount of gender identity or a larger amount gender identity, when the identity is described by male or female characteristics? This may seem to be merely a semantic argument; however, it appears that at its root gender identity theory is nevertheless grounded in the biological categories of male and female.

Identity advocates describe someone whose gender identity is congruent with their birth sex as cisgender (cis = 'on the same side'), being the vast majority of people. The gender movement maintains that the prefix 'cis' be used with nouns woman or man as in 'cis woman' or 'cis man' to differentiate those for whom their identity and sex match. We prefer the plain biological description; one is a 'woman' or 'man' based on sex characteristics, rather than supposed gender identity determining a person as a type of woman or type of man. All such descriptions are merely categories (or types) of gender identity, not a spectral dimension of identity.

For biological scientists like us, the ever-increasing catalogue of gender identity subgroups claimed to be on a spectrum is perplexing. For example, Abrams (2019) describes 64 gender identities. The numerous labels are confusing and appear to amplify separateness rather than similarities between people, raising barriers to human understanding.

Further, in English-speaking countries recognition of gender diversity is now reflected in changed use of pronouns which are seen as part of someone's gender (not sex) expression. Common usage of sex-aligned pronouns is abandoned in favour of preferred gender pronouns such as them/they, he/him, she/her, ze/hir in many areas of social interactions. Workplaces and businesses institute policies and training sessions to guide correct usage in interactions because one cannot tell someone's gender identity merely from how someone looks. Warns one guide, 'When someone is referred to by the wrong pronoun, it can make them feel disrespected, invalidated, dismissed, alienated, or dysphoric (or, often, all of the above.)' (Duke University, Office for Institutional Equity).

Confusion sometimes arises around the meaning of the term 'sexual orientation'. This concept may be mistakenly thought to be the same as gender identity. One's sexual attraction refers to which sex one is romantically attracted. A person may be sexually attracted to the opposite sex (heterosexual) or the same sex (lesbian, gay, bisexual) or to neither (asexual). One's sexual attraction (lesbian, gay, bisexual) is not gender identity. Transgender individuals can be gay or straight or bisexual/fluid. We should be clear that the concepts of one's sex (a biological binary), one's sexual attraction (lesbian, gay, bisexual), and gender identity (multiple) are distinct features. In recognition of different genders, official documents in some Western countries such as Australia, NZ, UK, Canada, and the European Union have introduced gender category options such as M, or F or 'neither'/ 'non-identifying'.

Most children become conscious of sex between the ages of 18 months and 3 years and correctly label themselves, 'I am a boy', 'I am a girl', and learn that a boy has a penis, a girl has a vagina. Very young children use external cues of clothing and hairstyle to decide the sex of others – a woman dressed in a suit with short hair is called a man; a man in a dress and make-up is called a lady; a boy wearing a dress is labelled a girl. The androgenous, gender-neutral fashion models of today are often incorrectly identified as male or female by young children. In typically developing young children, changing gender is common in dress-up play. They believe outward features such as clothing, shoes and hair style makes you someone different. It is reasonably common for some girls to dress, and behave as boys, as for some boys to dress and play like girls. These stages may truly be described as gender non-conforming or currently as 'gender-creative' play, as children are adopting the persona and behavior of the opposite gender.

By around 7 years of age typically, one's sex (gender)

identity becomes stable, whether it be gender conforming (stereotypical expectations of play and behaviour) or whether the child is 'gender creative', non-conforming (the tomboy girl, the effeminate boy). For girls, the feminist movement rallied to breakdown stereotypical expectations and open wide non-conforming opportunities in dress, education, careers, and sports. Gender theorists claim that a child's true gender is their internal gender identity that emerges over time, irrespective their physical body. Gender critical academics claim that the existence of a gendered 'soul' is an unproven hypothesis imbued in belief and psychology. The argument goes "how does one know what it 'feels like' to be a man or a woman when one 'is' simply a man or a woman".

What is Transgender?

Transgender people are those whose gender identity is not congruent with their natal sex. They are usually born with typical male or female anatomies but feel as though they're born into the 'wrong body'. Transwomen are those born biologically male and transition to identify as a woman. Transmen are those born biologically female and transition to a man. To reiterate from the introduction, we use two alternate labels throughout the text. The first is the singular nouns of transwoman and transman which denote a type of trans person, not a type of woman or man respectively. The second label is 'trans identifying male' as an alternative to transwoman. Although this latter label is eschewed by gender identity advocates, we believe this is a biologically true description of this subgroup of males. Using either preferred label underpins our perspective that a woman is someone born biologically female, with XX chromosomal makeup. Transgender identity is expressed via dress and lifestyle, name change, and pronoun use. Changed gender identity in some countries is by self-identification, with no requirements for sex-reassignment surgery or cross-sex hormone therapy (such as the gender recognition certificate). In many Western countries transgender people can now change their identity on legal documents (birth certificate, passport, or name change).

According to the American Psychiatric Association *Diagnostic Statistical Manual of Mental Disorders* (DSM V, 2013), transgender individuals feel a 'strong and persistent cross-gender identification and a persistent discomfort with one's sex' from young childhood despite normal chromosomal makeup. This psychiatric diagnosis is now labelled gender dysphoria, previously, gender identity disorder (p. 451). Some clinical services such as the Monash Gender Health Clinic in Australia, reject that pathological descriptions of 'disorder' or 'dysphoria' be used to describe their clients, preferring 'gender incongruence'. This diagnostic term is from the WHO International Classification of Diseases (ICD -11).

For some, transitioning to the opposite gender begins in childhood via name, preferred pronouns, dress and gendered interests and behaviour. Medical interventions (cross hormone treatment and/or surgery) typically occur in late adolescence or adulthood. National laws vary about the age of consent for gender reassignment treatment. The prevalent model of care for gender dysphoric children, 'affirming their belief,' and the wide use of puberty blockers to reduce teenager distress with puberty is under scrutiny in many countries because such approaches do not have a validated research base. The origins of one's sexual attraction and gender identity are inconclusive and multifaceted, with neither genetics nor specific social factors solely implicated.

Prevalence

The prevalence of transgender individuals is unknown and difficult to accurately verify as methods of collecting the census information and gender labels vary between countries. In some political cultures, the concept of gender diversity is not even acknowledged to exist. Where there are attempts to count the prevalence, different labels and the stringency of definitions used in surveys creates disputed counts for transgender prevalence. Some current estimates place the proportion of people self-identified as transgender or gender non-conforming at between 100 to 2000 per 100,000 among adults (Goodman et al., 2019).

In earlier decades, gender dysphoria was more prevalent in adult natal males but curiously recent data indicates ever younger cases and rapid growth in the numbers of teenage girls in comparison to teenage boys seeking treatment for gender dysphoria in Australia, the UK and USA (Zucker, 2017). There is a new term for cases whereby teenagers at puberty declare gender dysphoria with no previous childhood history– rapid onset gender dysphoria. A 2023 survey of parents reporting possible cases of rapid onset gender dysphoria in their children revealed that the 1655 adolescents and young adults were 75% natal females, were on average 14 years at onset (almost two years younger than natal males), and were more likely to have already taken steps towards social transition than natal males, 66% female compared to 29% male (Diaz and Bailey, 2023). A question about gender clinic location indicated the international makeup of this sample - 75% USA, 10% Canada, 10% Europe, and 5% Australia. In the USA estimates of trans in youth has doubled to 1 in 5 adolescents (aged 13 to 17 years) identifying as trans (Herman et al., 2022).

Prevalence data differs with the definition. For example, Collin and colleagues (2016) demonstrated that as the definition became stricter the number of cases reduced. From comparing 27 studies they revealed the highest prevalence in the self-identified group at 355 per 100,000; those undergoing surgical or hormonal therapy was 9.2 per 100,000; and the least numbers for the group having a transgender-related medical diagnosis, at 6.8 per 100,000. Other estimates show minute numbers ranging from 1.4 to 10.6 per 100,000. International comparisons are quite uneven. In Australia, the compulsory National Census of 2016 pinpointed 1260 respondents who selected their gender as 'Other - please specify' (not M or F), at 4.6 per 100,000 (with 5.5% TW and 7.5% TM within that group). A 2018 survey in Canada found that 0.24% of people aged 15 and older (approximately 75,000) identified as trans or non-binary. And a 2021 survey in Brazil of a representative adult sample of 6000 found much higher prevalence - 0.69% (690 per 100,000) identified as trans and 1.19% (1190 per 100,000) as non-binary (Spizzirri et al., 2021). Although accurate data are hard to come by, the prevalence of transgender is very low overall, although referrals to gender clinics in the USA, UK and Australia by adolescent girls in particular have shown sharp increases in recent years despite many presenting without any earlier gender identity issues (Kenny, 2020).

Childhood to Puberty
Hormones and Physical Changes

In brief, sexual differentiation under genetic and hormonal influences create biologically distinct physiques between males and females, beginning in-utero from 6 weeks gestation, continuing with dramatic development of secondary sex characteristics in puberty, and finishing with physical and sexual maturity in adulthood. Exposure to different concentrations, timing and mix of sex-aligned hormones, testosterone in males and estrogen/progesterone in females, produce contrasting effects on all cells of the human male and female body. These hormonal differences ultimately drive the physical development and sporting capabilities of male and females (described in detail in Chapter 3).

Testosterone, an anabolic tissue-building hormone, is released across the human lifespan but in vastly different volumes and timing between the sexes. Table 2.1 shows testosterone concentration levels increase with age in both boys and girls but that beyond childhood, the concentration in males far exceeds that in females. In puberty, males release testosterone mainly from testes whereas females release primarily estrogen/progesterone from ovaries, along with minor traces of testosterone from ovaries and adrenal glands.

At puberty, the testes secrete 30 times more testosterone than pre-puberty, with circulating testosterone levels 15 times greater than a woman of any age. In males, testosterone levels released during puberty are between 3 to 10 mg per day whereas in normally developing females, testosterone levels never rise above 0.25mg (2 nmol/L) a day at any age across the lifespan. Beyond the development of primary sex characteristics in the embryonic and fetal stages (the male and female sex organs), testosterone and estrogen/progesterone interact with growth hormones to activate the development of the secondary sex characteristics. Secondary sex characteristics are the physical changes during puberty that distinguish male and female physiques. Females develop pubic and axillary hair, breasts, wider hip-shoulder width ratio, and fat deposition around hips and thighs. Males develop bodily and facial hair, deepened voice, prominent thyroid cartilage thickening (Adam's apple), muscularity, fat deposition pattern around the abdomen, wider shoulders than hips, and on average a stronger and greater skeletal size with longer limbs, larger feet and hands, and more pronounced jaw. The development in puberty results in a sexually mature human, one capable of reproduction; menses in females and sperm production in males.

Table 2.1. Reference ranges for circulating testosterone (T) in healthy males and females of different ages.

Age	Male (nmol/L)	Female (nmol/L)
7-10 years old	0.06 to 0.20	0.09 to 0.36
13-17 years old	7.22 to 17.23	0.58 to 1.09
19 years and older	9.20 to 32.02	0.52 to 2.43
Post-Puberty Handelsman, Hirschberg and Bermon 2018 – Range values are upper and lower 95% confidence limit	7.7 to 29.4	0.06 to 1.68

Source: Sissons (2021) and Handelsman, Hirschberg & Bermon, 2018)

Note: serum testosterone concentrations are highly dependent on the immunoassay method used, creating difficulties in standardizing lower limits of testosterone concentrations (Handelsman, Hirschberg & Bermon, 2018, p. 806).

In adulthood, the testosterone concentration distribution for humans is bi-modal, non-overlapping, and widely separated for the sexes. The gap between the testosterone distributions is typically around 8 nmol/L (See Figure 2.1 below). But as both Handelsman and colleagues (2018) and Schultz (2019) indicate, using testosterone as the key to determine 'femaleness' in sport is controversial. Circulating testosterone level at any point in time is affected by many factors for both sex groups - exercise and exertion, time of day, even within same-sport, same sex athletes.

Male testosterone levels drop after vigorous exercise so that doping tests post-competition typically record testosterone at the low end of the range. However, as females lack androgen uptake receptors in their cells, their tissues have low androgen sensitivity. Therefore, acute effects of circulating testosterone on female physiology and performance is nullified even though their natural level might be measured higher than regulated. Nonetheless, long-term external administration of testosterone to females results in considerable androgenization of musculature, as was evidenced in the physiques of female East German athletes and their athletic dominance in the 1970-80s. Read Franke and Berendonk's (1997) in-depth revelations of the GDR doping program and effects on its athletes. Being a performance-enhancing anabolic steroid, testosterone, its precursors, and masking agents are on the banned substance list of the World Anti Doping Authority (WADA).

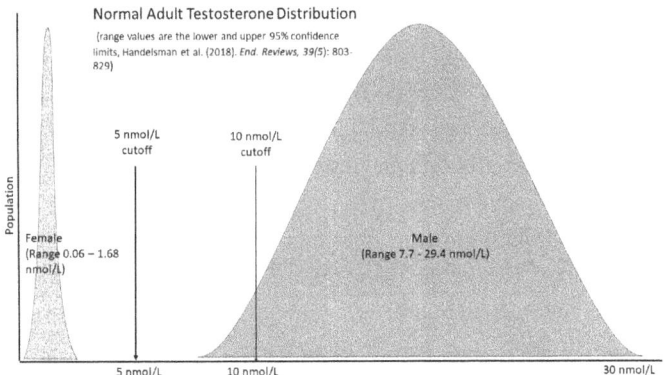

Figure 2.1. Testosterone distribution for typical non-menopausal female and male adults, showing cutoff levels in sport transgender inclusion policies.

Based on data: Handelsman, David et al., (2018). "Circulating Testosterone as the Hormonal Basis of Sex Differences in Athletic Performance." Endocrine Reviews, 39(5): 803-829. Doi:10.1210/er.2018-00020. Note: Hilton and Lundberg (2018) report that for non-menopausal females the typical testosterone concentration ranges from 0 to 2.0 nmol/L blood whereas in males it is 7.7 to 35 nmol/L.

In the trans sport literature, two arguments are commonly put for abandoning testosterone testing for trans athletes. The first is that because testosterone levels do overlap between some male and some female athletes, and secondly because testosterone level does not predict sport performance within a sport, testosterone levels should not be used to exclude an athlete. The research by Sonksen and colleagues is often cited to support these claims, however these research findings are often misrepresented. Yes, it is true they reported that 1 in 4 male athletes had testosterone levels dipping into the female range, and that 1 in 20 female athletes had levels rising into the male range. However, the data showed mean testosterone concentrations for each sex were still well separated. Furthermore, when looking at male and female athletes, none of the average testosterone levels for females overlapped with males for the eight sports common to both sexes – the female vs male average was 1 to 4 nmol/L compared to 13 to 25 nmol/L, respectively. Therefore, comparing like-sport-for-like-sport, the testosterone levels of male and female athletes show the distinctive bimodal testosterone distribution.

The most common medical therapy for transwomen athletes has been the administration of cross-sex hormones and/or testosterone suppression. The influence of these female-like hormones is to partially re-sculpt the male physique to become more 'feminine' by softening the skin, hair, voice tone and pitch, reducing muscle definition and bulk, and re-distributing cutaneous fat distribution to somewhat mirror the female body fat pattern. It is important to note however, that while hormonal therapy does appear to 'feminize' a male physique the effects of male puberty are retained, including skeletal size, limb length, hand and feet size, muscle bulk, ligament and tendon strength, and a larger heart-lung system. In the next section we review those changes in more detail and discuss implications for a natal man competing in sport against a natal female.

Transition Treatment

Transition refers to the process that trans people undergo to reflect their gender identity. Transitioning treatment is for life unless the individual de-transitions or desists. This process may begin in childhood, adolescence, or adulthood. Some individuals express their desire to be a different gender from early childhood, while many children and youth resolve their gender dysphoria. Reliable data on rates of de-transitioning (or desisting) is unknown, though some reports reveal rates around 2% to 8%, with evidence pointing to females who desist settle as lesbians, and males as gays.

Currently, for children the primary model of care of gender identity confusion is to affirm and support the child as being trans along with their self-chosen identity. This means letting the gender nonconforming (gender creative) child to dress, play and be named as they desire. For some trans children, medical intervention may begin with administration of puberty blocking hormones in puberty to delay unwanted physical changes associated with their natal sex, and to ameliorate the associated mental health distress and anxiety of being in the wrong body. This treatment is increasingly being scrutinized and is considered non-evidence based.

What constitutes best medical practice treatment of transgender youth is still unresolved, with concern that hormonal treatments are experimental, with drugs being administered 'off-label' (i.e., drugs are administered without clinical evidence of their safety or benefits for the treated condition). Legislation outlawing practices or treatments deemed to dissuade gender transitioning and called 'conversion therapy' have been passed in Australia (e.g., in the state of Victoria) and the UK.

Concerned clinicians point to evidence that autism spectrum disorder, depression, and anxiety may be comorbid conditions in young people with gender dysphoria. For children and adolescents with multiple mental health issues these clinicians argue that psychological counselling should be central to the treatment of the young person, to better understand their dysphoria, the treatment choices ahead and the risks. Criticism of treating dysphoria as the main and dominant issue without also addressing the mental health issues are growing. Young people and others such as parents relying on trans social media may be misinformed into thinking that puberty blockers, cross-hormones, and surgical treatments are safe and reversible. Instead, surgery is complex and irreversible, sexual pleasure is often impaired, infertility is common, and osteoporosis in young adulthood is common due to the withdrawal of testosterone in transwomen.

In Australia, with the advent of the gender identity movement, sporting bodies have been urged to provide affirmation and psycho-social support for transgender and gender diverse children and youth. Participation guidelines facilitate inclusion of trans children and youth (post 12 years). Children may play in the sex category with which they identify, use gender aligned locker rooms, and wear sports uniforms of their gender choice. Some adolescent guidelines permit trans youth to self-identify into the category of their choice without medical intervention and wear the sports uniform of that gender.

In some sports, transgender youth athletes must meet physical benchmarks for reasons of safety to other competitors or themselves, for example youth rugby. Participation in the girls' division by trans identifying boys undergoing puberty is more fraught as their rapid increase in physical capabilities creates an unfair advantage. We have already mentioned the high school athletes Miller and Yearwood, whose participation in high school track events winning most titles between them over several years, was permitted under the Connecticut Interscholastic Athletic Conference rules. There were no impediments to their participation. Self-declaration of their female identity was sufficient.

The case of transwoman swimmer Thomas, who competed for the University of Pennsylvania in 2021-22, illustrated the performance advantage in female sports in transitioning after male puberty. Despite having been ranked in the mid-400s as a male swimmer during the first three years of college, Thomas now ranked first in the female division having won multiple races. While NCAA regulations permitted trans athletes to compete as long as they had undergone at least 12 months of testosterone lowering treatment (the level was unclear), genital surgery was not required at that time.

As an aside, serious concerns were raised anonymously by natal female competitors and their parents about Miller and Yearwood's inclusion in Connecticut high schools' girls track events. A court case was mounted by three families on behalf of their daughters claiming illegal bias. The case was subsequently dismissed on a technicality because by the time the case was heard both trans athlete defendants (Miller and Yearwood) had graduated from high school, and no remedy could be made.

In this case, the complaint of bias was made on several grounds – the unfairness of unequal competition being uppermost, but also lost opportunities, being told to try harder to make the final cut, being demotivated because of no chance to win, and finally privacy concerns in having to share change rooms with male bodies.

In the court of public opinion, the debate rages. Those raising genuine questions about trans inclusion being unfair have been called transphobic, bigoted, disrespectful, reactionary, and misogynistic among other labels by the trans lobby. Some of those supporting girls' sport characterize trans athletes as cheats and frauds. In the background, sports' governing bodies have their gender diversity participation policies but rarely engage in open debate to either defend their policies or engage in reflective discussion on the current controversies. Revisit Chapter 1 and Appendix A for information on sport policies for transgender in various sports around the world. Also, Appendix B catalogues the feats of a growing number of openly transwomen in world sport.

Testosterone and Transwomen Transitioning

The key argument for inclusion of transwomen in female sport is that because testosterone is lowered in transition, they no longer have an unfair advantage competing against natal females. Trans advocates argue that lowering of testosterone removes any residual difference in bio-physiological and performance advantages. They also claim that transwomen's physical capacities are reduced to be near parity with natal female athletes and thereby are matched for fair competition. The regulated testosterone levels in sport transgender policies are built on these assumptions. As a first step to deciding the veracity of this claim, you might wish to look back at Figure 2.1. It illustrates the stark differences in typical testosterone distributions for adult male and females. To verify this argument longitudinal studies tracking changes in transitioning athletes are required. Unfortunately, such empirical studies are rare.

The earliest study relied upon to answer the question of performance parity following transition was by Joanna Harper in 2015. She presented data on nine sub-elite transwomen distance runners, herself included. The study compared their previous race times as men with their times now as women. The pre to post transition race times, when converted to World Masters' rankings, were similar. On face value Harper concluded that transwomen athletes did not carry over a performance advantage and therefore parity was proven. The results informed the IOCs 2015 transgender policy that decided on a testosterone cut-off of 10 nmol/L for transwomen athletes.

However, there are several important flaws in the Harper study which undermine the parity conclusion. There was no comparative, age-matched natal female group to compare the trans times with at those same race distances post-transition. Did training drop-off or did it increase over time? At what age was transitioning begun for each athlete? Were the hormonal protocols used in transitioning comparable or how did they differ? What were the actual measures of the maximum and minimum time changes for each athlete? Finally, why were only the averages of ranks and times reported? Answers to those questions would add greater robustness and clarity to the Harper conclusions.

A more recent study by Harper and colleagues (2021) addressed questions of when peak physical changes occurred during transitioning and what degree of change could be expected. They reported that while hemoglobin levels reduced quite quickly to natal female levels (within 4 months), other physical measures, such as muscle strength, lean body mass, and muscle area were still greater than females, even after 36 months of treatment. Further, other studies of transgender bio-physiology show that in the mature male body, measures such as hip to shoulder ratio, arm reach, hand and feet size and overall height, remain unaffected by transitioning treatment.

The summary by Pike and colleagues (2021) of these findings can be seen in the graph below. It illustrates the magnitude of changes that might be expected in male physiology after 12 to 36 months of testosterone suppression and cross hormone treatment. The highest percentage reduction was for thigh muscle area and grip strength, yet most other features had low to modest reductions. Of key importance, the percentage advantage retained by transwomen over natal females in physique or muscle factors ranged from 13% to 41%. Such a gap in high performance sports is still sizable and unlikely to be closed by natal female athletes, regardless of how hard they train, how motivated they are, the coaching expertise, or personal endeavour.

Figure 2.2. Summary of bio-physical changes in transwomen following testosterone suppression for at least 12 months

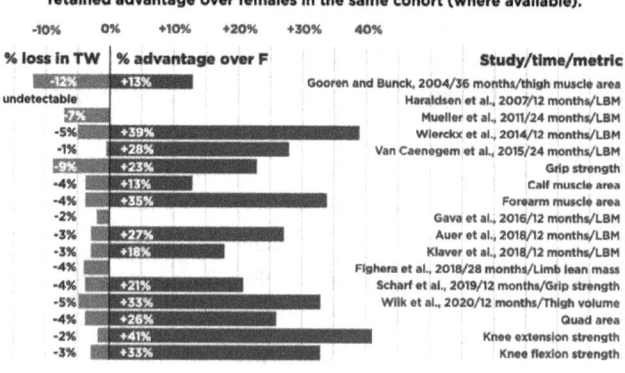

Source: Pike, Hilton & Howe (2021). "Fair Game: Biology, Fairness and Transgender Athletes in women's sport." Macdonald-Laurier Institute. Used with permission

Physique however shows persistent 'legacy effects' of male puberty which are not alterable with testosterone reduction. While studies are limited, these few studies indicate that the parity argument for transitioned transwomen compared to their female counterparts after 12 months of testosterone reduction is overstated. Such biological findings are instructive, with initial transgender inclusion regulations set at 12 months now being considered an insufficient time to 'wash out' male biological advantage. Recently revised policies have increased the duration for testosterone reduction in post puberty transwomen to at least 36 months, for example World Aquatics and World Athletics (Refer to Appendix A).

Finally, although transitioning does weaken transwomen athletes physically, there is also evidence that physical training has a protective effect on the male physiology when testosterone is low.

Firstly, the concept of muscle memory in physical training may explain the re-gaining of muscle strength capability lost during transition therapy. While original muscle fibres atrophy, adaptation occurs from physical training, muscle fibres are re-boosted, and muscle regains additional strength over time.

Secondly, beyond the sports science literature, physical training is shown to maintain strength in cancer patients. Androgen deprivation therapy in prostate cancer patients reduces testosterone availability to castrate levels (zero). To avoid negative physiological effects, regular physical exercise is a recommended adjunct therapy. Aerobic, strength and flexibility exercise programs have been shown to improve muscle mass, strength, and functional performance and reduce the risk of metabolic syndrome, cardiovascular disease and type 2 diabetes in men with very low or zero testosterone. Although much transgender transition research has been with non-athletic samples, athletic transwomen who continue to train would likely retain greater physical and performance capacities than their non-athletic trans peers. Trans athletes would benefit from sports training during transition, accruing at least similar physical benefits as shown in clinical populations.

It is relevant to point out that bio-physiological studies on trans children or youth athletes are lacking. Therefore, we do not know whether there are meaningful physiological, brain, or behaviour legacy effects when hormonal manipulations occur earlier or later in male puberty. Transgender youth present unique challenges, especially in representative rather than recreational sports, as teenage girls would be pitted against increasingly strong muscular male bodies undergoing puberty. Few sports, including the 2012 IOC framework, address youth participants' needs, and most are silent on restrictions around age of transition, or required protocols. However, Cricket Australia transgender regulations do not require trans youth players to meet the testosterone restrictions specified for adult players. World Aquatics permits a female identifying boy to compete in the female division if they complete hormonal transition prior to the onset of male puberty.

In the following chapter we continue the examination of sex-differences in biological parameters - the physique, function, and performance, as well as psycho-social differences. The data presented provide on-average comparisons between natal males and natal females, and between transwomen and natal female athletes.

CHAPTER 3

Females are Not Merely Males with Lower Testosterone

Having understood the genetic basis of sex in humans, and the role of sex-aligned hormones, especially testosterone, to growth and development of the male body, what does research say about the benefits that accrue for sports performance? In this chapter we consider the differences between the sexes in physical, functional, motivational and sport performance. This exposé will highlight that the female is not merely a male body with lower testosterone. Her physiology is fundamentally distinct from the male and related to specific reproductive function. Importantly, by making these comparisons, we do not feed an argument that the male sex is superior (male hegemony in sport is often condemned in feminist literature) but to highlight that these biological differences do matter in sport, especially in judging whether a contest can be fair. Further, we anticipate this information will provide pause-for-thought as to the rightful existence in the first place of female sport as a protected category of sport, devoted to athletes of the female sex.

Physical Differences

As described in the previous chapter, testosterone is an anabolic hormone and in concert with human growth hormone is responsible for tissue growth. At puberty, its release from male gonads results in dramatic and advantageous effects across the lifespan for the male compared to female not only in physique, but circulatory, and neurally.

Prior to puberty, same-age boys and girls on average differ minimally in their physical features. Junior mixed-sex teams and sport competitions are common and uncontroversial; boys and girls can compete equitably and as neither sex has a physical advantage competition is deemed fair for both sexes. Traditional boys' sports such as the football codes and cricket have included girls in mixed-sex teams for some time. However, with the advent of elite female leagues, the number of girl only teams is exploding.

In reverse, rule changes enable boys to now join mixed-sex teams in traditional 'female' teams sports such as netball. And as the number of male players has increased, male only teams and leagues at youth and adult ranks have developed for this former 'female' sport. Compared to post-pubertal males, the physically mature female skeleton is on average lighter and shorter by 12-15 cm, with correspondingly shorter limbs (levers) and smaller hands and feet. Females have a smaller pelvis to shoulder ratio, smaller and slimmer muscles (lower power and strength, especially in the upper body) and proportionally greater fat deposition, and different distribution around breasts, hips and thighs (lower centre of gravity). A wider female pelvis increases the Q angle between the femur and tibia (16 degrees compared to 12 degrees) which has been linked to greater injury risk at the knee compared to male athletes. Some evidence points to six-times greater risk of knee injuries in female soccer players, for which the menstrual cycle is also co-implicated. Strength training targeting the hamstrings and muscles surrounding the knee joint can mitigate the risk.

Cardio-vascular measures are also different. Females have lower haemoglobin levels affecting oxygen carrying capacity of blood, require greater dietary iron intake to buffer menstrual loss, and have smaller heart and lungs capacity in absolute terms. Overall, lean body mass (which affects power to weight ratio) is lower on average for both non-athletic females (79% vs 92%), and elite female athletes (on average 15% lower than the elite male athlete). Height-for-height, or weight-for-weight, the female biology does not produce the same physical output as a natal male. These physical differences summarized by Pike and colleagues in their review Fair Play (2021) are illustrated below in Figure 3.1.

Further, there is neuroanatomical evidence that the presence of androgens create differing neural pathways and brain architecture in males. Males appear to have a greater number of motor neurons, and larger neuron bodies. With the number of neurons inherited and fixed, it is conjectured that males have a post-natal advantage. However, the now better understood 'plasticity' of neural networks emphasizes experience and practice as key factors in the ultimate functioning of the nervous system and diminishes hypothesized sex-differences.

Figure 3.1. Sex-based percentage differences in physical characteristics (+ve % equates to higher male values/advantage; -ve % Equates to Higher Female Values/Disadvantage).

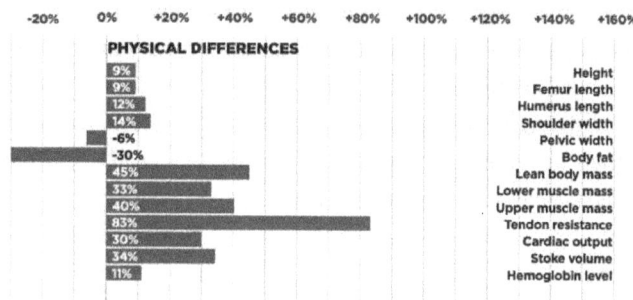

Source: Pike, J., Hilton, E. & Howe, L.A. (2021). Fair Game: Biology, Fairness and Transgender Athletes in Women's Sport. Macdonald-Laurier Institute.

Although trans researchers argue that these physical differences are not relevant to the debate of transgender inclusion because they are not about transgender individuals, such 'on average' biological differences are immutable in human males who experience puberty. Images of transwomen cyclists, footballers, swimmers, track athletes named in our Appendix B are readily sourced on the internet. These athletes have transitioned post puberty and their male physiques have not shrunk to be like their female competitors. Matching female and male athletes for physique (weight/height) in the same sport reveals the unequalness of performance, an example shown below in Box 3.1.

Box 3.1
Levelling the Playing Field? Physique Matching

Argument by transgender advocates:

"Because athletes differ in their biological and environmental strengths and weaknesses aside from sex, therefore gender identity cannot disrupt something [the level playing field] that never exists in sport."

BUT sex differences between matched physiques do matter.
Same height and about same wingspan:
USA swimmers Missy Franklin and Ryan Lochte
Height = six feet two inches tall; Wingspan of six feet four inches.

US swimmer and multiple Gold Medallist Missy Franklin. World record in the 200m backstroke, 2:04.06, set at the 2012 London Summer Olympics.

US Olympic swimmer Ryan Lochte's world record of 1:53.94, set at the 2008 Olympics in Beijing, was a full nine seconds faster.

Head-to-head, Franklin at her best would have been about half a lap behind Lochte at the finish, even though they are the same height and have just about the same wingspan.

"In a world in which competitors were categorized by height and wingspan—or just height or just wingspan—instead of sex, Franklin would not have had a world record; she would not have been on the podium; in fact, she would not have made the team. In those circumstances, we might not even know her name."
Source: Coleman (2017, p.90).

Functional Differences

In untrained or moderately trained individuals, clear functional differences emerge between males and females because of the anabolic effects of testosterone. Males possess greater heart and lung volume compared to females, which in turn differentially favor maximal oxygen uptake and endurance performance. Greater lean body mass, muscle bulk, and muscle fibres provide greater strength and power capacity. Further greater upper body musculature compared to females is a specific advantage in throwing, lifting, and arm sports. Considering neuro-muscular functioning, an increased output is achieved from a combination of a higher number of muscle fibres and neuromuscular synapses in males. Finally, some mental dispositions (mood, motivation, aggression) appear sensitive to testosterone.

Separately, these average sex-aligned anthropometric, muscle power and force, cardiovascular capacity and metabolic differences increase athletic capacity but taken as a whole, the combined effect is a competitive performance advantage of males over females. We reiterate - sex differences in power, speed and endurance should not be ignored in sport performance. These muscular and cardiovascular functional differences are illustrated in Figure 3.2 below. It is important to note that the sex dichotomy in reproductive and basic physiology and mental effects underscores that natal males regardless of gender identity, never experience such physiological challenges affecting optimal sport performance that natal females do.

Figure 3.2. Male-female functional differences (+ve% equates to higher male values/advantage)

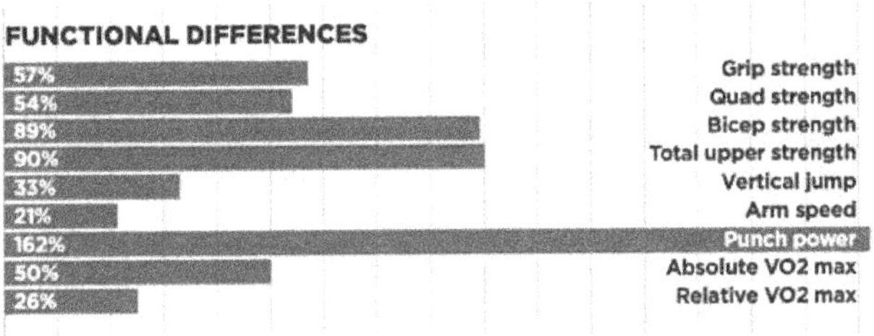

FUNCTIONAL DIFFERENCES

%	
57%	Grip strength
54%	Quad strength
89%	Bicep strength
90%	Total upper strength
33%	Vertical jump
21%	Arm speed
162%	Punch power
50%	Absolute VO2 max
26%	Relative VO2 max

Source: Pike, J., Hilton, E., & Howe, L.A. (2021). "Fair Game: Biology, Fairness and Transgender Athletes in women's sport." Macdonald-Laurier Institute. Used with permission.

Performance Differences

Although physically pre-pubescent boys and girls are similar, surveys of skills and fitness in children under 11 years consistently report boys' gross motor skills, strength and muscularity are on average more developed than girls, especially in ball skills (striking, throwing, kicking and catching) and jumping (for example, Ulrich, 2019).

In a series of meta-analyses involving 64 studies and 31,444 participants aged between 3 to 20 years, Thomas and French (1985) demonstrated that on average from early childhood, boys significantly outperformed girls in many motor tasks, including dash, sit-ups, long jump, grip strength and shuttle run. Ross Tucker has highlighted the divergence in male-female world track record times for events ranging from 100m to 800m. From ages 5 to 10 years when running times were similar beyond 10 years, boys' times in the same event were progressively faster than girls. Figure 3.3 below illustrates a similar finding based on current international age records (up to February 2022) for the 100m dash and long jump. With the onset of puberty, the male-female divide in physical performance increases markedly.

Figure 3.3. Age group world records for the a) 100m dash, and the b) long jump (8 to 18 years of age)

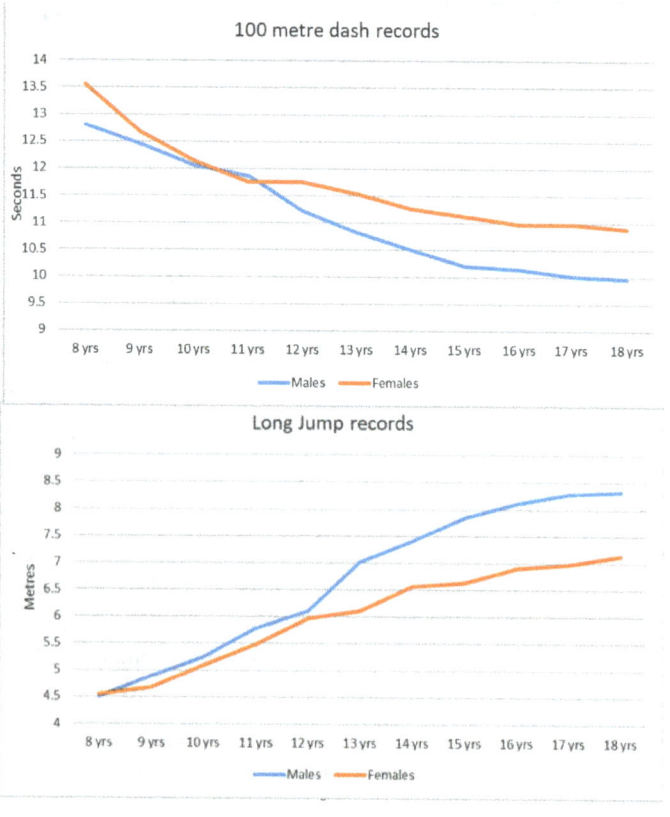

Across childhood in boys, upper body strength sports show a similar expansion of athletic prowess. From early puberty, powerlifting difference between the sexes increases markedly (see Table 3.2).

Table 3.1. Percentage difference in powerlifting by boys compared to girls (n=630, total weight lifted by boys ÷ girls)

8- to 9-years	10- to 11-years	12- to 13-years
98 %	115%	124%

Source: US Powerlifting TUE Committee Report (2019).

In adulthood, sex differences in the bio-physiological measures relevant to sport become magnified. On average, whether untrained or moderately trained, natal males have from 9% to 83% advantage over natal females in physical capacity. Sport-specific comparisons highlight male performance advantage more clearly (See Figure 3.4). Although the performance gap varies with sports, it is greater than 10% in all instances where speed, strength or endurance is tested. For running, swimming, rowing events, the average male advantage ranges from 10-13%; for kicking, jumping and throwing events, 16-22%; for striking events 29-34%; and for baseball pitching, field hockey flick at more than 50%.

Figure 3.4. Male-Female performance differences vary with sports

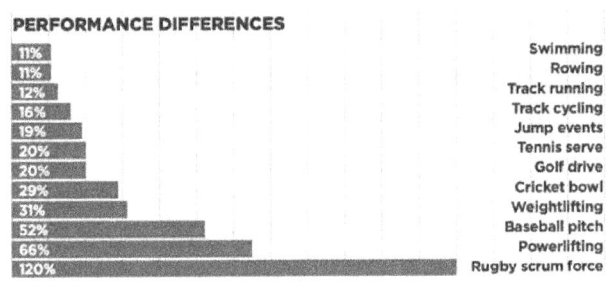

Source: Pike, J. Hilton, E. & Howe, L.A. (2021). Fair Game: Biology, Fairness and Transgender Athletes in women's sport. Macdonald-Laurier Institute. Used with permission

To elaborate further, the performance gap in Olympic weightlifting is dramatic. Males lift 30% more in both the 55kg and 69kg groups, and 39% more in the top/open group. Data between 2011 and March 2018 from all 1,300 International Power Lifting and affiliate competitions, and collated by Pike and colleagues, showed that the total weight lifted across the respective classes for Open female competitors (n = 6,351) ranged from 112kg to maximum 654kg (average = 305kg). Males (n = 11,000) lifted from 75kg to 1,105kg (average = 556kg).

When adjusted for physique size (similar body weight and height), the total lift for males was 64% higher than for females. Statistical analysis showed in weightlifting, sex was the greatest variable affecting the total lift and that being male was increasingly advantageous for each increase in body weight category. Figure 3.5 below illustrates Olympic world record lifts for weight-matched male and female lifters. The record for the heaviest female powerlifter failed to match that of the lightest male lifter highlighting that male lifters have greater power output weight-for-weight.

From such data, one can conclude that without sex-segregated competition, natal females would not have a fair chance in any mixed sex lifting competition. Despite this, at the 2020 Tokyo Summer Olympics in the 87+kg class, the first openly transwoman athlete was eligible to compete. Lifting for New Zealand, Laurel Hubbard had retired from lifting as a male at age 23 years of age and returned to the sport at age 39 after transitioning. Hubbard met the testosterone regulations, qualified on performance with the fourth highest lift total and ranked 7th in the International Weightlifting Federation women's 87+kg event.

This performance was despite being 43 years old at the Tokyo Games, and almost double the age of her female competitors. A double gold medallist at the 2019 Pacific Games Samoa, Hubbard

Females are Not Merely Males with Lower Testosterone 61

failed to lift the qualifying weight at the Olympic Games. Hubbard was lauded as a role model for gender diversity, and post-Olympics was awarded 'Sportswoman of the Year' in 2021 by the University of Dunedin.

Figure 3.5. Olympic Weightlifting World Records for Weight Matched Male and Female Lifters (approximately same height)

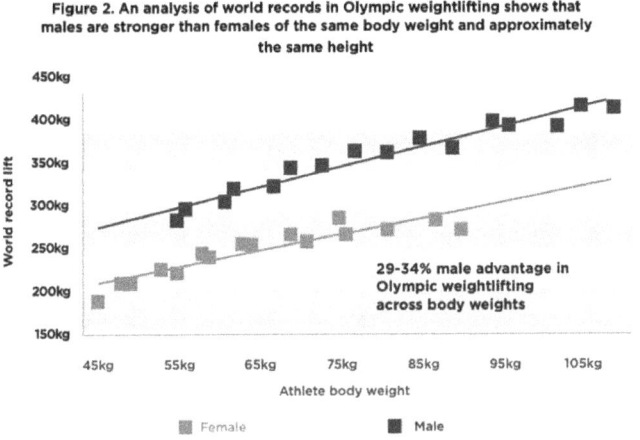

Source: Pike, J., Hilton, E., & Howe, L.A. (2021). Fair game: Biology, fairness and transgender athletes in women's sport. Macdonald-Laurier Institute. Used with permission.

The changes in world records since early last century in both swimming and 100m dash illustrate that there is still some way to go to close the performance gap between male and female athletes. For swimming, the greatest gains were in the years before WWII with modest and flattening gains in the years beyond 1980. In the 100m dash, female gains were most improved in the era between the two World Wars, except for an outlier time recorded in 1988 by Florence Griffith-Joyner. She was disqualified for this performance after failing a drug test. Since then, no other female sprinter has run close to that time, and the gap between men's and women's times no longer appears to be closing despite the extensive training resources now available to elite female athletics world-wide.

Figure 3.6. Sex gap in world records for
a) 100m freestyle, and b) 100m dash

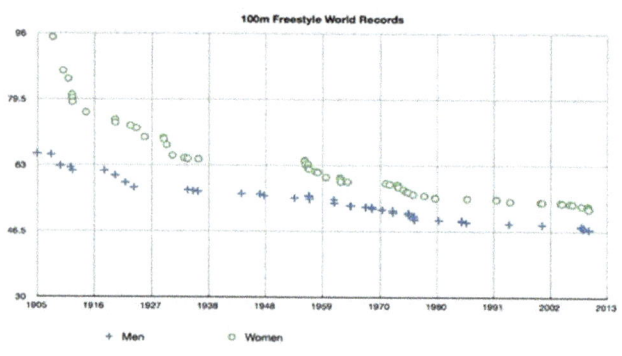

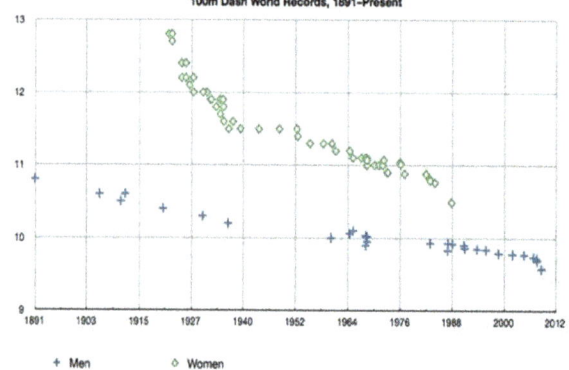

Source: Meyer, R. (2012). The 'golden ratio': The one number that describes how men's world records compare with women's. *The Atlantic*, 7 August 2012).

Finally, comparisons of the current world records for speed, strength and power events in athletics and swimming quantify the size of the male-female performance gap, being 4% to 16% depending on the event. See Table 3.2 below. There is some evidence that females may have performance advantages in ultra-endurance events and recovery, where some females are relatively competitive with their male counterparts. In such extreme sports, comparability between the sexes has been attributed to females' hormonal and evolutionary adaptation for endurance survival.

Table 3.2. Current male and female world records up to June 2023 (male ÷ female)

Event	Male	Female	Percentage female performance
100 m sprint	9.58 sec	10.49 sec	91.3%
Marathon	2:01.39 hr:min:sec	2:14.04 hr:min:sec	90.3%
Shot put	23.37 m	22.63 m	96.1%
High jump	2.45 m	2.09 m	85.3%
Long jump	8.95 m	7.52 m	84.0%
100 m freestyle	46.91 sec	51.71 sec	90.6%
1500 m freestyle	14:31.02 min:sec	15:20.48 min:sec	94.7%

Source: List of world records in athletics - Wikipedia

Overall, such performance data point to typical athletic male-female differences of between 10% to 12%, with most of the women's world record times falling outside the top 5000 times run by men. Sports statistics show that Paula Radcliffe's 2003 marathon world record run of 2 hrs 15mins 25 secs, was subsequently beaten by between 250 and 300 men per year. Coleman (2017) pointed out 'The women's 100m, 400m, and 800m records, which – unlike the marathon – are widely considered to be the product of doping, are beaten by literally hundreds of men each year, including by many high school boys' (p. 89).

The Rise of Female Olympic Participation

In most societies, sport is seen as a social good, an endeavour that builds national pride, a healthier populace, and social cohesion. Regular sports participation is seen to accrue mental, physical, and social wellbeing to all citizens. Today, most nations invest heavily in sport development, from grassroots to elite level, through physical education in schools, organized community sports, and talent pathways to nurture elite sports performers to compete on the world stage. The growth of female Olympians is a proxy indicator of the growth of wider female opportunities in sport.

It has taken many Olympiads for the number of female Olympian athletes to grow, with the ten percent mark not achieved until 1952 in Helsinki, and the 25 percent mark by 1988 in Seoul. The highest level of female participation was at the 2020 Tokyo Games, where almost 5,400 women competed (49 percent). In the 2020 games, 18 mixed-gender events in archery, athletics, badminton, equestrian, judo, sailing, shooting, swimming, table tennis, tennis, and triathlon were included.

Additionally, four International Federations moved to gender-balanced events for the first time (canoe, rowing, shooting, and weightlifting). There were three events exclusively for women; softball, rhythmic gymnastics, and artistic swimming; a number of mixed events, such as table tennis and badminton; and new mixed team events in table tennis doubles, shooting, swimming and sprinting relays. Other swimming and yachting events comprised equal numbers of males and females. Overall, women and men have always competed on equal terms in the equestrian and sailing events (although sailing has become increasingly segregated in recent years). New sports of Rugby 7s, surfing, skateboarding, and rock climbing added gender balanced events for male and female athletes.

In the Winter Olympics since 2014, more mixed team events have been added to the program, including mixed team aerials, ski jumping, snowboard cross and short track speed skating. Under specific gender equality initiatives of the IOC and international sports federations, the number of female (and mixed) events has resulted in the number of athletes competing in the Olympic Games rising to near parity for the first time (right and left panels, respectively in Figure 3.7 below).

Figure 3.7. Number of athletes (left panel) and events (right panel) by sex at the Summer Olympics from 1896 to 2022

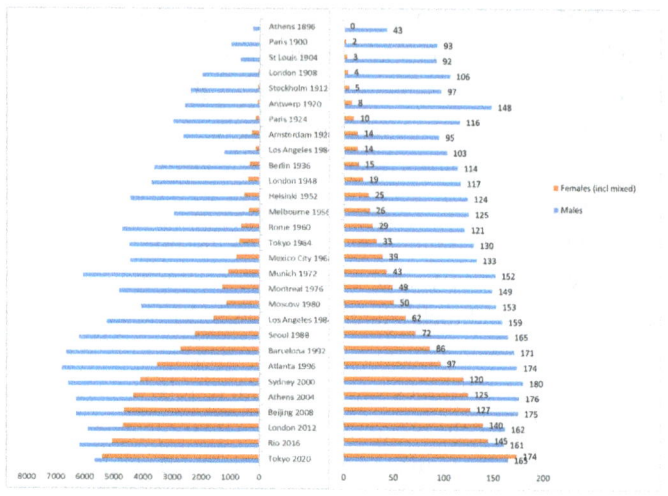

It is encouraging that in many countries, female sports now attract participants of all abilities, cultures, aspirations, and ages. However, as the sports industry developed, the inclusion of women in sport was not automatic. Nationally, organizations such as the UK Women in Sport, Sport Australia and Title IX in the USA have developed policy and governance to increase female participation rates in all aspects of sport – officials, governance leaders, and players. The 1972 Title IX legislation (see Chapter 1) in the United States provided significant impetus to gender equality by mandating equal funding to girls' high school and college sports programs. However, in recent years the inclusion of adolescent trans females in US school athletics has questioned who gets to benefit from Title IX. A legal discussion by Coleman in 2017 points out that "adopting sex blindness in competitive sport has the perverse effect of enabling non-elite boys and men to win spots and championships from elite girls and women" (p. 97).

Unique Physiological Challenges

It should be clear to the reader that testosterone level alone cannot define the female. It is not merely the absence of testosterone that makes a female. Females are not males with a uterus nor are transwomen females with a penis. We emphasize that females are biologically distinct from males and face unique physiological challenges when participating in elite sports. These challenges are mainly due to the sex differences in hormonal profiles, body composition, and anatomy. Briefly we list:

1. Menstruation: Menstruation can affect an athlete's performance, especially if it is heavy or accompanied by abdominal cramps. The menstrual cycle and irregularities may affect peak performance due to pre-menstrual bloating, pain and discomfort of menses, and fatigue. Intense physical training can lead to amenorrhea, or chronic anemia.

2. Hormonal fluctuations: Women experience hormonal fluctuations throughout their menstrual cycle, which can affect their energy levels (strength, power, and endurance), mood, and physical performance. For example, estrogen levels can affect a woman's ligaments, making her more prone to injury during certain phases of her menstrual cycle.

3. Pregnancy: In the modern era of sport, both pregnant and post-partum women have competed at the elite level, for example tennis greats Margaret Court and Serena Williams. Female athletes must finely adapt training routines and

intensity to accommodate the energy and nutritional demands of the growing fetus. The hormonal changes that occur during pregnancy can also affect an athlete's performance. Most sports, especially team sports where physical contact can occur, have guidelines about safety and health for competing pregnant athletes. In these sports, competition is often contraindicated by the third trimester. Many athletes continue physical activity to within days of delivery.

4. Body composition: Women typically have a higher body fat percentage than men, which can affect their performance in sports that require power-to-weight ratios, such as in gymnastics or distance running. Eating disorders are more prevalent in female athletes striving to maintain an ideal body type, often denying the physical changes due to puberty or the high energy demands of training and competing.

5. Bone health: Female athletes are at a higher risk of developing bone-related injuries such as stress fractures, compared to male athletes. This is due to factors such as lower bone density, hormonal fluctuations, and menstrual irregularities.

6. Heat regulation: Women tend to have a smaller body surface area and a higher percentage of body fat, which can make it more challenging for them to regulate their body temperature during intense exercise in hot environments

7. The 'female athlete triad' syndrome: Female athletes and coaches must be wary of the effects of high intensity training – a negative energy imbalance, coupled with lower estrogen levels and consequential amenorrhea (cessation of periods), which adversely affects bone resorption and lowers bone density. Stress fractures and injury result from this syndrome. Natal female bodies are designed to conceive and bear children, and the body interacts in uniquely different ways with intense physical training compared to transwomen athletes.

8. Nutrition in female athletes. It is highly important to provide the necessary fuel for high intensity training and competition. Reports of the increasing prevalence of eating disorders in female sports where athletes are required to conform to a narrowly defined body-image, such as swimming or gymnastics, highlight the insidious influences surrounding the "ideal" female body, and especially when elite squads comprise impressionable young and adolescent girls.

9. The energetic cost of reproduction. It is much higher in females. Obviously, male or transwomen athletes do not have to 'fuel' ovarian and menstrual cycles, let alone gestation and lactation as mothers. Some females begin high level training within weeks post-partum. Ukraine player Elina Svitolina returned to the WTA tour in April 2023 after giving birth the previous October.

10. Endometriosis. This is a chronic, debilitating disease caused by tissue similar to the uterine lining growing outside the uterus. Sufferers typically experience several long-term symptoms such as severe pelvic pain, heavy or irregular periods, infertility, bowel or urinary tract symptoms, and both physical and mental fatigue. There is no definitive treatment. For athletes, recovery may take longer, and higher iron intake is necessary to compensate for excess iron loss.

Transwomen athletes' male reproductive biology has a lower energetic demand, and close monitoring of training or competition demands is unnecessary. Testosterone fuels their biological development. Whether there are body image issues and related eating disorders in transwomen athletes requires further research. It's important for female athletes to receive specialized training, nutrition, and medical care that take into account these unique physiological challenges to optimize their performance and minimize the risk of injury.

Unique Social Environmental Expectations

Unfortunately, research studies have consistently reported a high attrition rate of girls from sport around puberty. Consistently, overall physical activity levels are lower in girls than boys and decline more rapidly with puberty. As early as 1993, an extensive review of literature by James Sallis identified that males are 15-25% more active than females from a young age, and female activity levels decline about 7.4% per year, compared to males at 2.7% per year. Two decades later, others such as Cairney and colleagues (2014) corroborated this trend and noted that arresting this decline in adolescent girls continued to be a public health challenge.

The decline in adolescent females' physical activity has been attributed to both biological and environmental factors. Puberty for girls presents many biological changes and challenges to participating in physical activities and sports. Not only issues surrounding menstruation, but many girls experience more negative body image problems, largely driven by unrealistic comparisons in social media.

Environmental factors include lack of access to facilities, safety and transportation issues, social stigma, a decreased quality of experience and access to resources, cost, risk of injury, and lack of positive role models. Consequently, for many sharing change rooms and toilets, and having to disrobe or shower in the presence of a male-bodied transgender girl/woman can be very confronting. Since her recent competition experience, Riley Gaines, the female swimmer who ran second to transgender swimmer Thomas in college swimming, has become a vocal opponent of transgender athletes in women's sport and their incursion into female-only spaces such as change rooms.

Some girls are adversely impacted by cultural or religious factors. Restrictions on interacting with males may be taboo, and the presence of trans girls may be unacceptable. Recently, concerns regarding sharing overnight accommodation with trans identifying males, for example on school, college or girl-guide camps has caused girls to either self-exclude or be withdrawn by their parents concerned for their safety. Forcing girls to share spaces with males, where they are asleep or in a state of undress, is a known and recognised safeguarding risk. Nancy Hogshead Makar, Olympic Gold Medallist, is a vocal critic of the transgender incursion into female sport. She stated, 'Girls and women shouldn't have to give up their hard-won opportunities, no matter how real the harms suffered by transgender athletes'.

On the other hand, transgender advocates argue that such biophysical comparisons are not valid because they are not specific to transgender athlete issues. At times, it seems to us that it is as if transgender women deny that they have inherited a male body or that their transitioning was solely about identity and not a change of their natal biology. Trans supporters also contend that because some individual natal women athletes are bigger, stronger, faster, and perform better in some sports than do some individual natal men, and because elite women athletes may outperform most untrained men, this is evidence proving that natal females are not disadvantaged in mixed events. We beg to differ.

As Tucker (2016) and others emphasise, no female could reasonably hope to succeed in sports against the significant physical advantages, without sex segregated events in most competitions. Sailors stated in 2020, 'If sport is a mutual quest for excellence, then participants should have a reasonable chance of winning' (p 2). Female sport has always been a closed category to uphold fair competition among members within that eligible group, those born genetically XX. The next chapter addresses the issues of fairness and safety in sports and to what extent these priorities can be upheld with inclusion based on gender identity rather than biological sex.

CHAPTER 4

Unintended Consequences for Female Participation

Integrity is a central pillar for fair sport, without which sport loses its authenticity, its meaning, its reputation, and value to society. It is crucial to players' and spectators' enjoyment and to society's confidence in the contest. Universally, sporting bodies spend much effort in regulating to prevent unethical behaviours such as doping, match-fixing, or corruption that manipulate results giving rise to unfair advantage, unfairly skewing the playing field, and dishonest performance.

Sport New Zealand includes participant safety and fair treatment as part of integrity, encouraging positive sporting cultures that foster enjoyment, mental and physical health, and safety. Importantly, all involved in the sport industry at whatever level or role – the athletes, administrators, officials, supporters, and other stakeholders, on and off the sporting arena are responsible for upholding positive behaviours underpinning sporting integrity.

Such standards of integrity should also necessarily apply to female sport. The conduct, regulations, and processes must be fair, in order that female athletes have confidence that their competition is a level playing field. Despite this, the supposedly 'unproblematic' act of grouping athletes by gender identity in competition undermines this confidence but only for female athletes. The basic integrity of their competition is undermined if transwomen participate because of the male athletic advantages related to their physiology. And it is telling that the concern for integrity is not shared across the whole of sport, because the male category is completely unaffected by gender identity grouping. Male athletes retain their superiority in a contest against transmen (natal females). This 2022 statement by Lia Thomas points to her sense of entitlement to competing as a female "No one should have to choose between being who they are and participating in the sport they love".

Such asymmetry in negative consequences from gender identity grouping in sport goes beyond the integrity of female competition. There are other consequences, rarely researched or discussed, for girls and women athletes arising from transwomen inclusion in the female category. This list is not exhaustive. We address a) weakening female sporting motivation, b) whose voice is heard, c) usurping female sport achievements, d) female role models, e) sporting careers and rewards, f) doping ethics, and g) case-by-case applications.

a) Weakening Participation Motivation

Thus far, the transgender inclusion debate has rarely considered effects on the motivation of females to engage in and persist with sport and physical activity participation. Participation motivation derives from complex factors with both biological and societal origins. It requires an understanding of what females want from their sport and the degree to which sport is central to their being. Research is rare on such issues, however anecdotal instances from the past several years from female athletes point to negative impacts.

The case of UK Cycling and the dominance of a trans rider Emily Bridges came to a head in 2022. Female riders took on the governing bodies of cycling, UK Cycling and UCI (International Cycling) and their unfair inclusion regulations. Natal female cyclists felt their sport was being taken away from them by subterfuge and that their rights and efforts in female sport was disrespected. Without action, UK cycling was faced with a potential boycott by female riders. It was forced to backtrack by suspending their transwomen inclusion rules for review. Tellingly, these threats of boycott represented the frustration felt by riders that their sport authorities wrongly assumed female riders would merely acquiesce to this new 'reality' of transwomen participation.

The disquiet among female athletes is building from other instances in elite female sport that we have previously described, such as, the admission of trans swimmer Lia Thomas in US college swimming and trans weightlifter Laurel Hubbard representing NZ at the Tokyo Olympics. From the beginning of the new regulations permitting male incursions into female sport, female athletes have expressed bewilderment. They have been hesitant about sharing their competitions, and their changerooms and unsure how to proceed. That these concerns have been made anonymously and mostly off the record, is indicative of the pressure from authorities within their sport for the females to put their feelings aside and comply. Their uneasiness often stems from making the rights and feelings of transwomen (although a tiny minority) a priority against those of natal female athletes (the vast majority). Oppressive coercion is reported by many who oppose gender identity ideology. Female athletes have a right to feel upset when they can see how their personal dedication and years of sacrifice to get to the top in women's sport, in the end, will come to nought competing against a transwoman competitor.

The probability of success from years of effort and hours of training in sport is an important factor in maintaining motivation. Motivational theorist Susan Harter points out in her 2012 book that while learning from failure is adaptive, facing repeated failure with no possibility of success leads to learned helplessness and withdrawal. Whilst being accorded 'underdog' status (a diminished chance of success) can be highly motivating in some elite athletes, insurmountable barriers such as a male-bodied competitor is likely to produce humiliation and hopelessness

Though having the talent and the drive to develop her skills, Connecticut high school track athlete Chelsea Mitchell expressed feelings of helplessness when confronted by trans girl competitors. Against such competition, she felt that all her hard work to reach her peak potential in competition was futile. She expressed the view that every loss to a transwoman athlete is demoralizing and that with every loss, it gets harder to try again (reported in The Daily Mail, 28 May 2021). Hannah Arensman, a former champion cyclist who lost out on a podium spot to trans rider Tiffany Thomas, announced her retirement from the sport because of the recent increase in transgender athletes competing in women's cycling. "At my last race at the recent UCI Cyclocross National Championships in the elite women's category, I came in fourth, flanked on either side by male riders awarded third and fifth," she said in her retirement announcement. "My sister and family sobbed as they watched a man finish in front of me, having witnessed several physical interactions with him throughout the race." (www.iconswomen.com)

Such anecdotal reports appear to point to demotivation and helplessness if adolescents face perceived unfairness. A serious question arises: will the advent of transwomen inclusion hasten female sport drop-out through lack of success or reduced motivation? Would such perceptions deter girls from even joining sporting teams in the first case? There is little formal research involving natal female athletes which shows that participation motivation would be boosted or not affected by trans inclusion.

Teasing out the motives for participating in sport and physical activity is complex. It varies with stage of life cycle, the type of sport, one's motor skill level, and one's sex. Suffice to report, several studies over the past three decades such as Allender and colleagues in 2006, and Soares and colleagues in 2013, on the motivational factors reveal divergence in motives between males and females. Such studies show that adolescent males participate for competition and success, and that sporting success builds their status. Males identified strongly with 'to be a sport star/ champion', 'to be popular' and 'liking competition.' Adolescent females seek social aspects, friendships, sociability, and fair play in sport. For highly physically active girls, skill achievement, increased self-esteem, improved fitness, and friendships were important motivators while ongoing participation centred around relationships and their personal image of being feminine and attractive to boyfriends. As could be expected, some motives are common to both males and females – the social motives of fun and enjoyment, being part of a team, as well as health and skill motives. Importantly, such motivation research was framed in the context of single sex sport experience for participants, not gender identity. Anecdotal accounts of young women's distress at encountering trans competitors point to discouragement rather than motivation.

In seeking to unravel causal relationships in differences in motivational style and sports interest between male and females, Deaner et al., (2016) chose an evolutionary biological explanation. While they could not discount the role of socialization, they attributed prenatal hormones as having an important role in the expression of different competitive modes between men and women, especially in same sex competition (in an evolutionary sense).

Accordingly, they posited that competing men were more likely than women to use high stakes physical aggression (e.g., fighting) whereas women were more likely to use indirect or relational tactics in expression of aggression. This account linked the influence of sex-related pre-natal hormones on the developing foetus as being fundamental to emergent sex-differences in motivational styles, especially testosterone in males. We do not yet know whether such basic differences are sex-linked through life or whether they are mitigated by one's gender identity. The next issue is closely related to motivation, whether one's views on matters of concern are taken seriously, respected, and action taken.

b) Whose Voices are Heard?

Transgender participation is only controversial in the female category of sport because of the demonstrated advantage from the male biology of transwomen (see Chapter 3). It is clear that the push for inclusion of transwomen athletes in female sports is polarizing among coaches, and competitors alike. Yet, it appears that the views of natal female athletes, those directly affected by these so-called progressive policies, are rarely sought or listened to. Some have been censored by the press, others have been warned by their sporting bodies or universities to remain silent. That coercive attitude alone should be sounding alarm bells.

With little empirical research, natal female athletes' views are not really known beyond growing anecdotal reports. While female and male elite and Olympic athletes' voices are rarely heard in the socio-political discourses of academic literature, Devine's 2021 research of the views of 19 female Olympians is enlightening. Most of the athletes in her study felt that they could not discuss the issue openly for fear of accusations of transphobia even though they said they were not hostile to transwomen athletes. Anecdotally, when natal female athletes have spoken out, they have been confronted by censorship and vitriol, often threats of violence. While not indicative of wider views, social media has been used as a weapon to destroy reputations. Anna Vanbellinghen (Belgian Olympic Volleyball player) fears lifechanging opportunities for natal females being taken away due to the admission of transwomen athletes into female competition, and a sense of powerlessness (Inside the Games Brian Oliver, 30 May 2021).

Female athletes appear concerned at the lack of scientific evidence in support of the assertion that including male-bodied athletes is fair play. Further it is unclear that females were even aware changes to participation guidelines were in train. For example, Paula Scanlon, a former teammate of Lia Thomas, explained in a June-2023 interview about the total lack of care or due process when the female U Pennsylvania swim team were told of Lia Thomas joining the female team. It was Thomas who announced her selection at a compulsory, pre-training meeting. It was a meeting called without forewarning of its purpose, and in which there was no opportunity for swimmers to reflect on what was being told, nor questions or discussion about how that could be.

In an open letter to the IOC on 13th December 2018 female Olympic athlete Ana Paula Henkel (Fair Play for Women https://fairplayforwomn.com) pleaded for the voices of female athletes to be heard.

She pointed out that denying biological differences in the name of human rights and political ideology undermined the considerable gains made by females in sports. She argued that the effects of competing against transwomen athletes went well beyond the missed rewards of podium finishes to much more damaging adverse psychological consequences and emotional costs on natal women. By no longer having equal opportunity to reap rewards of their talent and years of training effort Henkel claimed that the transgender polices in sport "repress, embarrass, humiliate" natal females.

The recent report from a survey of athletes, coaches and administrators undertaken by the UK Sports Council (2021) revealed that a large percentage of respondents sought anonymity for fear of backlash to their opposition to inclusion of TW athletes in female sports. Sports administrators or coaches were also fearful of losing their jobs if citing that their personal positions conflicted with the official ruling. Anyone arguing for women's rights to their own competition are labelled as transphobic. With such a prevailing atmosphere, hostile to dissenting voices, one wonders what purpose a survey would serve, other than reinforce the status quo and further discourage the expressing of genuine concern.

The mother of an Ivy League Swimmer told the Women's Declaration International Conference on 26 February 2022 of the bullying treatment of female swimmers by the University of Pennsylvania. She told of the formal letter sent to the members of the female swim team on the selection of trans swimmer Lia Thomas in late 2020. The letter pointed to the university's policy on inclusion and fairness, such that sex and gender were equal concepts (though they are not). It informed the team that Thomas' selection was legal under the current transgender guidelines (sports bodies capitulating to non-scientific claims). It warned that dissent, public comment, or questioning of this selection could lead to de-selection and loss of athletic scholarship (open threat). Mandatory team meetings silenced discussion (no debate). Team members with any concern had to raise it through the coach or athletic director (who had power to de-select for dissent). The swimmers were told their priority was to protect their trans team member yet their distress at this unimagined situation was disregarded (one-sided care). Understandably, the mother remained anonymous to protect her daughter's identity, such were the severity of university's sanctions for disclosure and dissent.

This account was recently corroborated by one of the U Penn swimmers, Paula Scanlon, in the YouTube clip "You will regret it!" recorded in 2023. She has decided to speak out about a flawed process. Parents who expressed concern over their daughters' anxiety were advised to seek psychological counselling, and their athlete daughters offered social re-education programs by the university to adjust to the new reality, according to Scanlon. The rules governing transwomen swimmers have thankfully been tightened since the release of World Swimming's policy. For now, trans swimmers who undergo male puberty are barred from competing in the female category. This change has put an end to Thomas' bid to trial for the US Women Olympic swim team, a bid denied on the grounds of unfair physical advantage and the truth of biological science.

While Title IX in the US (see Chapter 1) was designed to equalize funding and opportunities for female sports in US schools and colleges and advance female sport, the access of transwomen athletes to competitions or funding set aside for female athletes is being challenged in the courts. For example, Selina Soule is one of three female runners who brought a Title IX complaint against the State of Connecticut for the NCAA transgender inclusion policy. Soule's case rested on competing human rights, either fairness for natal females or inclusion for transgender athletes - while transwomen athletes should be treated fairly, their opportunities should not be at the cost of discriminating against a natal female. Coleman (law professor and former elite 800m runner) and Donna Lopino (sports consultant and former head of US Women's Sports Foundation) judged that Soule and other natal female athletes had a case on the basic principle of sex-based funding. However, others such as Elizabeth Sharrow (2021) accuse those who defend sex-based rights of twisting the principles behind Title IX by denying the human rights of female identifying male athletes.

'Third wave' feminism validates transwomen being women and trans girls being girls. This so-called 'intersectional feminism' claims that any move in sport that is good for transwomen is also good for all women. Therefore, by this position women's sport should become 'gender expansive' in order to reap the greater benefits. As Sheree Bekker stated in 2022, "Sport isn't inherently gendered ... we manufacture strict binary gendered differences, then we naturalise them... Inclusion is not only the right thing to do, but it also makes us all better... I will always fight for the inclusion of trans women in women's sport".

Not surprisingly, feminists of an earlier era call out such claims as risible and repudiate the claims that advancing the rights of a subset of men identifying as females can bring beneficial change for all women. Former tennis champion Martina Navratilova has voiced allowing transwomen athletes in female competition as 'insane' and 'cheating', comments that have been labelled transphobic, although she was coached for a time by notable transgender tennis coach Renee Richards. Feminist philosopher Kathleen Stock also opined that a women's rights movement is not concerned with advancing male privilege, and that in denying that binary sex exists in humans, the gender identity movement has resorted to emotional manipulation rather than accepting facts of biology.

The controversy surrounding the dominance of celebrated trans cyclist Emily Bridges was a catalyst for female riders to stand up and be heard. In April 2022, 76 current and former elite riders signed an open letter by the Union Cycliste Femine (UCI) that decried the rules that permitted transwomen riders in their events. The letter requested that the head of British Cycling's Olympic and Paralympic organizations demand action be taken by the UCI to rescind its trans inclusion rules. The riders demanded the authorities heed the unequivocal scientific evidence of physical advantage of natal male riders, accept that gender identity is irrelevant to fair cycling, and that the sport authorities uphold their duty to fairness for female athletes.

Of course, there are trans athletes who disagree that it is okay for transwomen athletes to play against females. Former Olympian decathlete medallist transwoman Caitlyn Jenner has spoken out in support of natal female athletes. She strongly rejects the view that she, like other transwomen, could compete fairly against natal women athletes, even with testosterone suppression. Even now as a Masters level athlete, Jenner refuses to compete against natal female golfers citing that it is grossly unfair. To quote, "I don't think biological boys should compete in women's sports – we have to protect women's sport… That's the bottom line." This view was also echoed by Australian trans cricketer Cate McGregor in an opinion piece in The Australian newspaper "There is no case for trans competitors at the elite level in women's sport. The difference in size and strength between biological women and trans women who have had the benefit of testosterone in puberty is too great" (24 April, 2022).

Male youth athletic championships will always be won by males, yet with trans inclusion in female sports a female youth champion may be of either sex, though likely be a male. Rather than embracing all who identify as women (natal males included) under the 'gender expansive' banner of 'third wave' feminism, gender critical feminists argue instead that the presence of transwoman athletes in the female category perpetuates sexism, fortifies traditional male power, and accedes to male wants rather than meeting female needs.

Indeed, Sharrow (2021), a US public policy researcher and political scientist, has characterized recent Title IX provisions and state laws banning transwomen from female sports as 'reframing sex non-discrimination as a means of gendered *exclusion*'. Her extensive analysis dismisses "sex as a binary" as fiction, in favor of the gender continuum. She argues that political institutions are in "cahoots" with medical authorities to advance, enshrine, and normalize 'cis-supremacist gender orders' and perpetuate the erroneous concept of binary gender 'normativity', rather than gender diversity. She asserts that biological sport scientists, gender critical feminists, and allies advocating for the rights of natal female athletes are transphobic, anti-trans activists on the political right, accusing them of "fuelling state-sanctioned return to cis- and heteropatriarchal gender order" (p.1).

It is little wonder that, rather than be seen as aligned with extreme reactionary groups or judged as transphobic, those most affected - the natal female athlete and their coaches - have remained silent. But it is important to consider that if all stakeholders are not consulted and engaged in any proposed change (radical as it is in this case in women's sport) and if there is no discussion of all perspectives then integrity in sport cannot be upheld.

Ironically, while in society at large women have been encouraged to speak out for their rights and expect to do so, with transgender in sport many female athletes are too fearful of the backlash if they do. Such a confronting climate of stifled debate and the unfairness of the change has negative implications for the motivation of females to take up sport in the first instance. Nonetheless, despite the toxic culture of bullying, some current, younger female athletes over the most recent year or so are speaking out against the unfairness of transwomen in their sport. For example, US swimmers Riley Gaines, and Paula Scanlon, and Australian Olympians Cate Campbell and Emily Seebohm have made public their views.

Women athletes need to be at the table arguing their views and defending their hard-won sex-based rights in sport. The messages from these female voices are as valid as transgender voices. The climate for open discussion and reasoned debate is essential. Women must have representation at the discussions about revision of participation guidelines, which inevitably will occur under the latest IOC framework principles.

As we see it, the past errors made in framing the sports' current partition guidelines that created an untenable situation for women's sport, was largely due to a narrow human rights perspective ignoring biological reality and being in the thrall of the ideological perspective of gender identity. To support any mooted change in participation guidelines research evidence should have been collected on the effects on natal girls' motivation with the inclusion of trans youth into their competitions. To date, it appears that their views have largely been at least ignored at worst suppressed and denied. If integrity in female sport is to be preserved, all stakeholders - female athletes, transwomen athletes, biologist, sport, and social scientists – together need to contribute to a fair solution.

c) Usurping Female Sport Achievements.

Contrary to statements that transgender athletes have a minuscule effect in female sport because of their insignificant numbers, and that there are no gold medallists among their number, we find dozens of examples over the past decade or so[1]. We describe several notable examples that point to tangible, negative consequences for natal female athletes. In sports where transgender rules are loosened, such as cycling, examples of male bodied riders in female events abound. Podium finishes are more common, and female riders are denied the results they deserve.

In swimming, the celebrated case of Lia Thomas has been covered several times in this text. We add this further information about her achievement in the female ranks. Thomas's rankings soared after transition from 554th (M) to 5th (F) in the 200-yard freestyle; 65th to 1st in the 500-yard freestyle; and 32nd to 8th in

---

[1]. See Appendix B on this book's website. The link to access additional online resources is provided at: https://doi.org/10.18848/978-1-957792-73-6/CGP

the 1650-yard free. Such remarkable improvement in the female events compared to the male events could not be attributed to more dedicated training across those few years and was accomplished despite testosterone suppression. Such improvement speaks for themselves – the biological advantage.

The Ivy League meet in January 2021 at Harvard created much consternation about whether Thomas was swimming on merit throughout the entire race or merely coasting, to then surge at the end. In the 200-yard freestyle which Thomas won in 1:43.12, she was even with runner-up Samantha Shelton (Harvard) at the midway point. But over the last 100 yards Thomas surged, highlighted by a 25.04 split for the last 50 yards. This closing split was faster than the finishing laps of Olympian Missy Franklin in her American-record performance, or the best closing effort recorded for other elite US swimmers Katie Ledecky, Mallory Comerford or Siobhan Haughey.

At the NCAA meet at Georgia in March 2022, Thomas contested finals in three events winning the 500-yard freestyle. She won that event by more than one second over Emma Nordin (Arizona State), with a time that was only 6% slower than her personal best in men's races (where typically the male-female time difference is 10%). The natal female who failed to make the final cut in any of these events or who swam 4th will forever be anonymous.

Reka Gyorgy, a swimmer on the Virginia Tech team, lamented on Thomas' win: "I know you could say I had the opportunity to swim faster and make the top 16, but this situation makes it a bit different, and I can't help but be angry or sad. It hurts me, my team, and other women in the pool. One spot was taken away from the girl who got 9th in the 500 free and didn't make it back to the A final preventing her from being an All-American. Every event that transgender athletes competed in was one spot taken away from biological females throughout the meet".

It is worth recalling that the opposite situation of transmen inclusion in male sports is not at all controversial – this situation does not hinder male sporting achievements. Transmen, because they are biologically female are not a physical match with natal males regardless of cross hormone therapy and have no superior physical advantage. Two examples of how uncompetitive transmen athletes were after crossing into male sports is telling. Schulyer Bailar swam for Harvard across the 2015-2019 NCAA seasons. His final 100-yard breaststroke swim in 2019 ranked only in the top 34% of all NCAA Division 1 swims for the season. Iszak Henig (Ohio State, NCAA season 2022-23) moved across to the Ohio State men's team for the 2022-23 senior season, placing from 69th to 79th in the 50-, 100-, 200-yard swim events in that season. It is clear neither swimmer challenged the status quo for their male competitors.

In sport, female champions and world record titles have been recognised in their own right, irrespective of the men's records within the same event. However, in this new era, given the evidence of physical and performance superiority of an elite transman athlete, future sporting records set by trans athletes are likely to set near-impossible benchmarks for natal female achievement. Will these times be considered authentic female records when set by transwomen athletes? Further, will aspirations of young female athletes be dashed when they compete against a transwoman athlete or when team selection is usurped by them? We do not know the views of the 21-year-old Samoan heritage NZ weightlifter who missed Olympic team selection for the 2020 Tokyo Games to a much older transwoman lifter, but other coaches and athletes voiced their anonymous incredulity that this could have occurred.

d) Female Role Models

Competitive sport has long committed to the women's category, to provide females with an equal opportunity to benefit from both direct and indirect advantages, and to showcase successful female athletes. Sporting role models are important to young girls' aspirations and female participation, e.g., US tennis great Serena Williams, Olympic swimmer Katie Ledecky, champion Australian athletes Samantha Kerr in soccer, Meg Lanning in cricket, Ashleigh Barty in tennis, or Lauren Jackson in Basketball.

However, without their achievements being separately recognized, none would be household names. Research into sport motivators reveal that effective role models are those that are 'believable' 'authentic' and 'credible'. Would transwomen athletes fulfil these requirements for natal girls? For example, the review by Allender and colleagues in 2006 identified that while gender stereotyping had a serious, negative effect for girls (by limiting their aspirations), realistic role models for all body types and competency levels were important to encourage girls into sport. The research showed that adolescent girls overwhelmingly nominated female role models, although fewer were from sports compared to those chosen by boys. Within the role modelling context, the phrase "if you can't see it, you can't be it" becomes relevant.

We acknowledge that this same argument could also be put by transgender people wishing to see 'their kind' in sport. It is clear that media promotion of transwomen athletes and their rise to celebratory status creates visible role models for their community. Trans and gender diverse people claim that to see oneself depicted in society affirms their existence and encourages them to get involved. For example, non-binary 1500m runner, Nikki Hiltz, a biological female wins a female race in July 2023. She is given exposure in media outlets and claims her win is for the LGBT+ community - that they can play sport and be a winner. However, being biologically female her win is nothing special, or controversial. She was simply the best runner in the race.

As brought up earlier, trans athletes such as weightlifter Hubbard are lauded as trailblazers and role models. In the context of transgender inclusion, the IOC's medical and science director Budgett, was quoted as saying "There is some research, but it depends on whether you are coming from the view that of inclusion as the first priority or absolute fairness as the nth degree" and "consider the fact that there have been no openly transgender women at the top until now [referring to Hubbard], I think the threat to women's sport has probably been overstated" (Saxby writing for *Fair Play for Women* in 2021)!

It is difficult to fathom that a male IOC medical and scientific director could hold such biased views against fairness. These astounding statements defy biological science. The argument of trans supporters that a 'tiny minority' cannot upset the opportunities of the majority is strongly rejected by women's sport supporters. It is not merely about the single trans podium finish. Every time a transwoman athlete is selected on a team, competes and/or wins is one opportunity lost for a female athlete right down the successive grades. Opportunities to participate are lost for girls and women. It's not about merely not being a winning athlete; it's about the lost opportunity to a level playing field in female sport at any level.

Further, media attention given to transwoman athletes in elite female competitions has stripped attention away from laudable achievements of females coming "second", and those excelling in other sporting events at the time. The great media stories of female endeavour and success loose out to the controversy. Research has yet to explore whether having transwomen athlete role models work for girls and young women, even though they may for transgender youth.

To be motivated to engage and stay in sport, young females need to see that female athletes with female bodies can achieve success in sport.

e) Sporting Careers and Rewards

It is encouraging that in many countries, female sports now attract participants of all abilities, cultures, and ages. Women's sport has finally found its visibility, having largely emerged from the shadow of 'sporting patriarchy' that restricted female participation and controlled sport in earlier eras. Sports aim to encourage females to join, to be motivated to stay involved, and if talented, to make the huge training commitments required to excel. The 2018 gender equality project report of the IOC stated the clear intent "…sport is one of the most powerful platforms for promoting gender equality and empowering women and girls" (p 2). As described in Chapter 3, the 2020 Tokyo Olympic Games was the most gender equal in history, with almost equal numbers of male and female athletes (49%). But in other areas of sport officialdom women were well underrepresented. At the Tokyo games only 13% of coaches were female and 31% of administrators or officials were female.

Women's sport around the world is growing fast. Australian women's teams are excelling at the international level in cricket, netball, basketball, soccer, tennis, rugby and others, and with female athlete contracts, and more equitable salaries, prize money and sponsorship, females can now consider a professional sporting career. A place in the talent pathway and team selections for young competitors are the first steps to these rewards, achieved with years of dedication, hard work, and some luck. The first case in Olympic history, of 43-year-old trans weightlifter Hubbard qualified in the Oceania bracket initially displacing the 21-year-old female athlete Kuinini Manumua. The much younger, natal female Manumua was eventually granted a special invitation to represent Tonga and placed eighth.

It is worthy to consider the selection dilemma faced by coaches of the near-future – should they take on and nurture over time a talented girl but knowing that her winning times will be broken by a transwoman competitor, or should they follow the pathway to almost instant success by coaching the transwoman athlete? What elite opportunities and financial rewards would be usurped in the future by this new category of participant in female competitions?

Part of the inspiration to become an athlete is that girls and women are able to develop careers both within and outside of sport by exploiting their profile. Through sport, female athletes are exposed to situations that benefit the development of both tangible and intangible, transferable professional skills that are essential to make them competitive with men in their professional lives beyond athletics – 'soft skills' such as leadership, teamwork, problem solving, tenacity, goal setting, commitment, dealing with disappointment, and so on. Such benefits have long been enjoyed by winning male athletes. An Australian example of opportunities for females, usurped under the guise of gender identity, are grants available in the annual Women Leaders in Sport scholarship programs offered by Sport Australia.[2] The first eligibility criterion for this female grant program is that applicants 'identify as a woman.' Hence identity is key, and thereby a male identifying as a female can 'read themselves' into a program with finite funding and one designed to advance opportunities and overcome traditional disadvantage for females within sport. This contradiction in terms makes the whole program – to promote women leaders – less effective.

---

2. Sport Australia (2023). *Women Leaders in Sport grants and funding program 2023.* https://www.sportaus.gov.au/grants_and_funding/wlis/leadership

Much of the controversy around transgender participation in female sport has been played out on the elite stage. Most defenders of the status quo argue that this is where sports integrity must be carefully managed. Most inclusion policies details what should happen at the elite level with detailed regulations around testosterone levels, duration of therapy, procedures, processes, and decision-making personnel. However, the issues about fairness and safety also resonate at the community level of sport. Trans advocates in Australia continue to push for transwomen competing in elite sport by the letter of law and insist that community sport should have a similar, albeit unlegislated, approach. As their argument goes, because community sport does not involve extrinsic rewards, prizes, or fame, female leagues or sports events should readily embrace and welcome transwomen to play.

Countering this dismissive claim ('it doesn't matter because there are no prizes'), defenders of women's sport strongly assert that it is not for men, or even those who identify as women, to decide what benefits women can enjoy from their sport. The demand is that only women should decide their own rewards, needs, or wants - this is sporting feminism, which fortifies sporting integrity for women.

f) Doping Ethics

In gender transition treatment, there is much import placed on hormone manipulation to modify the body to look more masculine (transmen) or feminine (transwomen). In trans youth, hormone therapy is used to either prevent or delay puberty; trans adults are treated with stronger, lifelong doses of cross-hormones. In sport, reduction of testosterone levels has been to diminish – but not remove completely - its effects on physical capacities and to supposedly close the male-female performance gap. However, under the latest 2021 IOC framework, testosterone suppression therapy is no longer mandated, unless deemed a medical therapy.

In spite of this, recently revised regulations do require testosterone levels as low as 2.5 nmol/L for participation in female sports. Research on the long-term consequences of such low testosterone on a healthy, athletic male body. Some evidence is emerging of chromic osteoporosis in young adult males who underwent puberty blocking and cross hormone therapy in the later years of their youth. Transgender treatment is lifelong. Under medical supervision, trans athletes of both genders are subjected to irreversible, therapeutic, cross-hormone treatment to achieve the physical changes aligned with their self-identified gender and so to meet eligibility regulations.

We also question whether medical administration of hormones, to otherwise physically healthy individuals, is within either the spirit or ethics of World Anti-Doping codes. In all other circumstances, regardless of which athlete in which sport category, testosterone as well as other anabolic steroids or precursor and masking agents are banned substances on the ever-increasing World Anti-Doping Agency (WADA) list. Administering testosterone to trans identifying female athletes on the face of it is in direct conflict with the ethos of 'drug free sport.' However, there is an 'out' for athletes prescribed medicines for health. When administered for medical reasons, athletes can avoid the strict doping protocols and drug sanctions by their sports medicos obtaining a Therapeutic Use Exemption (TUE) on their behalf.

Therefore, one could ask whether exemption sought for transitioning hormone therapy was ever originally an intended rationale for the TUE process, a process legitimately instituted to allow for relevant health care for typical medical conditions athletes may suffer. Logically then, with exogenous testosterone now a sanctioned treatment (with a TUE) and some sports deeming a particular accepted level of serum testosterone, could one now mount the argument that it is only fair to permit natal women athletes to artificially boost their testosterone level to match the higher hormonal benchmark applied to transwomen athletes.

Also, it could be argued that puberty blockers should be available for all athletes, not just restricted to the treatment of gender dysphoric girls or boys. In the gymnastics and diving disciplines, power-to-weight ratio is critical to complex rotation manoeuvres. Pre-pubescent bodies have optimal physique proportions for maximizing this capacity. Recognizing the reverse disadvantage to older (post-pubescent) gymnasts, the injury risk to immature bodies, the mental stresses, and distortion of the age profile of senior competitions by ever younger athlete competitors, in 1997 the International Gymnastic Federation set the minimum age for competing at senior level at 16 years of age.

Puberty blockers artificially enhance performance by delaying into the late teen years the physical changes in females, such as widening of the hips, and greater fat accumulations around hips. Such plausible, yet clearly unethical manipulations of natural growth, would further compromise the health of the female athlete and diminish the integrity of women's sport.

g) Case-by-Case Applications.

Worth mentioning is also the problem of unintended consequences of the administrative burden to sport arising from inclusive participation guidelines.

From a sports management perspective, one could expect that the major difficulties will not fall on professional administrators at the elite level of sport, although this level is where most publicity occurs. Instead, the burden will be greatest at the community level where 99% of sporting activity occurs and on the volunteer administrators.

At the elite level there are many resources to support the legal, scientific, financial, testing /authenticating and sanction requirements of the guidelines and policies. The current guidelines about process for the peak sports in Australia such as Australian Rules Football, netball and cricket, point to a detailed procedure to regulate trans competitors in a fair and confidential manner. These procedures require considerable investment and diversion of resources within the sport. The guidelines for the smaller, lesser-resourced sporting bodies are aspirational statements about inclusion and fairness. They are loosely framed and open to differing interpretations. Time-poor, often volunteer, officials in smaller sporting codes and community level sport are now being asked to administer a major change in participant eligibility without the necessary specifically trained personnel, financial resources, or legal advice backup to fairly balance legitimate concerns among all participants.

These latest IOC guidelines state that transwomen applications be treated on a case-by-case basis, predicated on individual assessment of disproportionate advantage and the applicant's right to privacy. However, on reading individual sport policies, it can be readily concluded that the procedures set out are highly bureaucratic and time-consuming for both applicant and the sport. Such applications require due process and procedural fairness and the effort to verify information, such as the authenticity of supporting documents, the vetting of the athletes' performance in the previous gender, or the safety risk the athletes' male physique could pose to female opponents. The requirement for transparency yet privacy, and the complexity of assessments of health and performance information by non-specialist (often volunteer) administrators make the task almost unworkable. Further, decisions of the sporting authority are necessarily subject to appeal which may involve costly litigation.

Therefore, a growth in case-by-case determinations will necessarily consume scant financial and personnel resources across sport. A 2023 ruling that transwoman basketballer Lexi Rodgers was ineligible to play elite level women's basketball by Basketball Australia, took a month of deliberations, and involved a panel of three experts – BA's chief medical officer, a BA board member, and a medical academic. However, many sports, particularly female sports, have smaller financial resources to draw on. Transgender inclusion policies now require a process for each individual transgender applicant. Balance that against rights afforded by biology, in accordance with sex discrimination legislation that made legal sex-segregated sport categories for those who have undergone puberty, and where physique, strength and stamina are relevant to fair play.

While it is welcome that in Australia, major sporting bodies indicate they will rollout 'how to' resources and provide training of sports administrators and club officials, one can ponder whether the information will address on-the-ground difficulties, and provide the practical support to officials, or even whether this essential training will be undertaken by busy volunteers. At the grass roots level, recruitment and turnover of volunteer officials is already a difficult task, without adding a complex layer of legalistic decisions about player rights and eligibility.

In conclusion, we question whether these seven consequences are indeed unintended, or could they be characterized as being blindly overlooked or ignored as unimportant. We speculate whether the current paradox in female sport could have arisen, if instead of a majority of male administrators, there were more senior female directors in sport, and that female voices were sought, and open discussions held in the lead up to inclusive policy formulation.

The concerns, needs and demands of female athletes for their sex-based category are only now coming to the fore, and such entreaties paint a very different picture to the gender identity approach. We argue that females in sport must be supported, and that the integrity of female competition be upheld if female sport is to deliver social good for participants. By our focus, the issue is not complex for sporting bodies. First, sports' governing bodies should ask themselves this clear question: For what purpose do we have a female category of sport anyway? The answer to that simple question will define what their policy response should be regarding either sex-based or gender identity-based sport.

We finish this chapter by concluding that the existing transgender policies do not stand up to biological scrutiny. In the end all want sport to be fair and safe, and for all to play sport at any level to do so in a socially safe environment free from harassment. Sports need to undertake the difficult policy work to shape a different way forward to include transgender athletes in sport.

Simply decreeing that one's gender identity is female, and that hormonal changes makes one equivalent to natal females is unscientific. Insisting that transwomen have a human right to the female category yet ignoring advantages of male biology is unscientific. To disregard the hard-won rights of generations of natal female athletes and to usurp female sporting opportunities, their recognition, and their achievements renders female sport meaningless to society. Girls and women will be the losers. Our clear call is that sporting bodies should suspend their gender diverse guidelines, reassess the biological evidence, and revise their guidelines accordingly.

CHAPTER 5

Competing Priorities in Sport: Balancing Safety, Fairness and Inclusion

Rights and Protections in Sport

Humans should have access to, and be free to practise physical education, physical activity and sport without discrimination based on ethnicity, gender, sexual orientation, language, religion, political or other opinion, national or social origin, property, or any other basis. The sentiments in the Box below show goodwill toward trans athletes to find their place in sport. It is within the spirit of the human right to play sport, explained in Chapter 1. Sports need to find a way to eliminate prejudice and unjustified discrimination.

I am fully supportive of trans athletes like Emily Bridges and Lia Thomas. However, I think it does sport a great disservice when people whose bodies developed with the strength, bone and muscle mass of males are pitted against people whose bodies developed as females. I hope a solution can be found that accommodates fair competition for all - and which allows us to celebrate trans athletes as real winners.

Reader comment: Daily Mail online 31 March 2022, *Trans cyclist Emily Bridges is BARRED by sport's international governing body from racing in women's national omnium championships against Dame Laura Kenny a month after competing in male events.*

However, we also know that in sport there have always limits on who may play. Participants must meet eligibility criteria for protected categories such as age divisions, weight divisions, disability, and the female category – this is justifiable discrimination. So, the right to play sport does not confer a right to compete if a person does not meet the eligibility criteria for that category. Yet, by disregarding biology in women's sport, recent sport inclusion policies have created conflicting rights in women's sport. Is it fair for females to have to compete against male bodies? Is it safe when bigger, stronger, more powerful bodies are playing? Can inclusion coexist with fairness or safety?

The male performance advantage we described in Chapters 2 and 3 is a fundamental reason for the female category in most sports and within sports, concessions have been made to the smaller, lighter physique of females. Rules have been adapted around equipment or matches, such as shorter tee boxes in golf, lower nets in volleyball, lower hurdles in athletics, smaller balls in basketball, smaller/lighter throwing implements in track and field, shorter boundaries in cricket, and fewer sets in tennis competitions. The range of events is more equal than ever. Such rule adaptations are rarely doubted in sport, although some question the need for fewer sets in tennis (equal prize money) or shorter periods of play. Such restrictions are seen as stereotyping female capacities as inferior and being anachronistic to gender equity.

Gender equity in sport is being achieved in several ways. Increasingly, international events host the same event for males and females to boost participation parity. An example is the addition of the Olympic 1500m swim for females. Some events, such as the equestrian disciplines, have always been mixed sex, with the sex of the athletes being irrelevant to the outcome of the sport contest. There is a call for sport to develop more nuanced responses to the inclusion of transgender athletes in female sports.

Safety, Fairness, or Inclusion: What are the Priorities?

The challenge for most sporting bodies is how to ensure the right to play sport is supported in a way that is safe, competitively fair, and inclusive for all. Some argue that transgender people should be able to take part in the sport category of their gender identity at every level with no restrictions. However, a tension exists between the relative importance of providing a safe or an inclusive environment for sports participation – we argue they are mutually exclusive, and certainly not fair for many sports. Biologically, when transwomen athletes compete against women, we are pitting male against female bodies. If we accept that there is no distinction to be made between male and female bodies, then the category of female sport per se ceases to exist.

Against the background biological information presented in earlier chapters and understanding that the male biological advantage is not removed in transitioning transwomen athletes, we have undertaken an analysis of sports from the competing priorities of fairness, safety, and inclusion. Table 5.1 categorizes common sports under one of these three perspectives - if natal females were to compete against a transwomen athlete in that sport or event. Is physical safety at risk, is competitive fairness at risk, or could the sport be played with both fairness and safety assured and thereby be inclusive?

According to the priority approach (Pike, 2020), we ought to test rules for safety, then fairness, and then inclusivity. Safety and fairness need to be prioritised over inclusion. Our analysis revealed that few sports could include transwomen athletes without compromising either safety or fairness, or both.

Table 5.1: Safety, Fairness or Inclusion:
What should be the priority?

Safety	Fairness	Inclusion
Australian Rules Football Basketball Boxing Cycling Fencing Gridiron Handball Hockey – field and ice Martial arts, e.g., taekwondo, karate, judo Netball Rugby Soccer Track skating	Artistic swimming Athletics – most track and field events BMX, cycling- road and track Climbing Cricket Dance sport Diving Downhill skiing, Mogul Gymnastics – all forms Kayaking, canoeing Luge, Skeleton Rowing Surfing Swimming Tennis, Badminton, Volleyball - any net divided games Triathlon Volleyball Weightlifting	Archery Croquet Darts Equestrian Lawn bowls Mixed relays (if conventional view of male and female) Motor sports Non-contact / adapted form of sports, e.g., touch rugby Sailing Shooting Snooker

Safety

Invasion-style ball games pit athlete against athlete in the same field of play and are usually based on the gaining or regaining ball possession to score goals. Rules of most of these team games sanction physical contests to dispossess the ball carrier, with varying degrees of permissible bodily contact. Sports such as Rugby, Australian Rules Football or American football involve frequent physical confrontation, grappling, and colliding. For example, the tackles, rucks, and ball contests involved in rugby confer an advantage to bodies that are larger and stronger.

In combative sports, such as wrestling, MMA or boxing, athletes must physically outpunch, out grapple, out kick to overpower their opponents for the win. The well-established physical strength, power, speed, and force production advantages given by testosterone during puberty despite transitioning (See Chapter 2) give transwomen athletes significant advantages over natal female opponents for these sports.

Where disparities exist in physical size, speed, power and force, the risk of injury is heightened for smaller, weaker, slower bodies. Although boxing bouts are weight classified, natal male athletes are still more powerful than weight-height matched female boxers. Therefore, player safety and welfare must become the foremost consideration for sports administrators. Even in combative sports, such as boxing, judo, martial arts where weight-based categories ensure a fair contest, the superior strength and power of males compared to female bodies in the same weight class heighten the risk of injury. There are several examples of natal females being seriously injured when contesting a transwoman. In 2014, transwoman MMA exponent Fallon Fox ended the career of her opponent, Tamikka Brents. Within the first three minutes of their fight, she shattered Brents' eye socket, an injury requiring seven staples in her head. In a TV interview Brents stated "I've fought a lot of women and have never felt the strength that I felt in a fight as I did that night. I can't answer whether it's because she was born a man or not because I'm not a doctor. I can only say, I've never felt so overpowered ever in my life and I am an abnormally strong female in my own right. Her grip was different, I could usually move around in the clinch against other females but couldn't move at all in Fox's clinch," (Whoa TV).

For sports listed in Table 5.1 under 'Safety', the risk of injury to natal women from transwomen inclusion is high. As presented earlier, even when testosterone has been suppressed for up to 36 months, the biological differences, and physical advantages remain (Hilton & Lundberg 2021). Several 'non-contact, invasion' team sports in which players compete for ball possession can also be listed under the safety category. For example, in hockey, basketball or soccer, despite rules of play against unfair bodily contact, there is still potential for less powerful, smaller and slower bodies (natal female against male bodies) to be injured in unintentional collisions.

The UK Sports Councils *Guidance for Transgender Inclusion in Domestic Sport* report in 2021 propose a 'hierarchy of contact' for grading sports for safety. The hierarchy from safest to least safe ranged from sports competing in parallel with zero contact (such as gymnastics, track sprints, or pool swimming), to contact sports (netball, basketball, football, hockey), to collision sports (both rugby codes) then combat sports (boxing, judo, karate). Such a grading potentially provides a clear viewpoint on physical safety of competitors which sports should carefully consider when determining what level of safety risk a transwomen competitor presents to a female athlete.

Fairness

The principle of fairness is the idea that all participants start on an even playing field and have an equal opportunity to experience success; and that inherent performance advantages (height, weight, muscle power, etc.) are randomly distributed among participants of the same 'category'. Sports listed in the fairness category are those where physical contact and a heightened injury risk are not necessarily present in the contest, but strength, power and physique are still performance advantages. These are essentially the sports which have traditionally had men's and women's divisions, for that very reason.

Such sports may be characterized to be testosterone-impacted sports. Athletes in these sports may compete separately one by one (e.g., field events such as discus), head-to-head in parallel lanes (e.g., swimming, running) or player v player (e.g., racquet, net divided sports). Within the same biological category, the athlete with the physique, strength and power advantage is more likely to win. With mixed-sex groupings there is not an equal opportunity for success. Natal females are still at a significant performance disadvantage if competing against transwomen.

Inclusion

The sports listed in the Inclusion category are those in which no advantage is gained if their elite competitors differ in physique, strength, or power. For many years some sports in this category have allowed males and female to compete head-to-head, for example, equestrian events such as dressage, and show jumping. To compete on a level playing field, the athlete's biology or the athlete's gender identity are irrelevant to the outcome of the competition; and fairness and safety priorities are assured.

Over the past decade, many sports have prioritized an inclusion perspective in their participation policies in response to advocacy by transgender and gender diverse allies. These policies have been framed around the valued concepts that recognition of one's gender identity and playing sport are fundamental human rights, but the policies also diminish issues of safety and fairness for women within their sports.

However, with the biological attributes of male-bodied transwomen athletes, even for those who have transitioned, a central question arises. Are the advantages afforded to transwomen tolerable or intolerable? Some women's sport advocates such as Coleman (2017) and Knox and colleagues (2019) conclude that while human rights underpin respect and acceptance, prioritizing inclusion based on gender identity creates an intolerable unfairness, and a potentially hazardous situation in female sport.

If self-identification is the rule, and anyone can compete in the category of their choice, then sports are risking both integrity and fairness in female sports. The impact of perceived or actual unfairness or safety concerns on young women's willingness to engage with sports is unknown. Embracing the principles of human rights and inclusion as priorities in preference to fairness and safety is the challenge for administrators of female sport at present.

Recent Changes in Transgender Policy

World Rugby. A Case Study

Women's rugby has grown rapidly in popularity around the world, with world cup events attracting positive media attention and sponsorship. Such developments, though important, are fragile and to nurture its growth World Rugby embarked on an extensive examination of how the IOC 2015 transgender policy could work in a contact team sport. They commissioned a review of the scientific literature and consulted with experts in a range of relevant areas.[1] This resulted in its 2020 Transgender Policy, the most stringent among contact team sports or football codes at that time.

The policy disallows transwomen from playing in the women's game if they transitioned after puberty and thereby benefitted from the biological benefits of testosterone. Their background evidence clearly pointed to a female being at physical risk if male bodies were introduced into their competition. In other words, in this case, World Rugby prioritized physical safety over inclusion. By contrast, Rugby organizations in Australia, New Zealand, USA and Canada have failed to follow this decision and have adopted the opposite position in their guidelines. Table 5.2 details the regulation differences. These national bodies permit transwomen players to compete in female teams if they undergo testosterone suppression and meet lowered testosterone benchmarks. As mentioned in Chapter 4, little is known about the long-term health impact on the transwoman testosterone levels are reduced to levels as low as 2.5 nmol/L. Nevertheless, the consideration of

---

1. Details of these consultations may be located at https://www.world.rugby/the-game/player-welfare/guidelines/transgender.

residual physique, power and strength in transitioning males and the injury risk to females in a collision sport like rugby continues to be ignored.

Table 5.2: World Rugby v Rugby Australia

World Rugby	**Rugby Australia**
Transgender women may not currently play in any women's rugby competition	Transgender women may play in women's rugby at the community level
Safety is a priority. The risk of injury to a natal female is too great	Everyone should be able to play, and inclusion is the right thing to do.
Decision based on scientific evidence about biological and physiological differences, the effect of testosterone suppression and later retention of meaningful performance advantage.	Decision based on human rights principles
Extensive research of available scientific literature, detailed and extensive consultation by the working group with experts in the fields of performance, physiology, medicine, risk, law and socio-ethics.	Consultation with past and present trans players and members of the trans community, Rugby Australia Member Unions and stakeholders, other sporting bodies, Pride in Sport, and internal individuals including the Chief Medical Officer, Legal and Integrity representatives, Coaching staff, and the Head of Diversity and Inclusion.

Interestingly, for the opposite situation of transmen (natal females) rugby players, the risk of injury was considered a concern. Regulations for transmen stipulate that they not be permitted to play until they had a 'sign-off' from a medical expert testifying they were sufficiently physically equipped and safe to compete in the male category.

Incongruously, the physical safety of female bodied players was taken seriously when playing in the men's competition, but the situation of the physical safety of female bodied players up against natal male players in women's rugby was not. Why might these other rugby governing bodies not use the research too? One of the exercise physiology consultants aiding World Rugby, Ross Tucker, claimed in a media report in April 2022 that while some rugby organizations agreed with World Rugby's stance, they were unwilling to change their current regulations to protect women's rugby because they were wary of a 'huge backlash' from trans allies and media. One reportedly said, 'it's not worth the blowback'.

How Have Other Sporting Bodies Addressed Inclusion Policies?

Because sports' governance is distributed among International, National, and Provincial levels, there are few uniform guidelines about transgender athlete participation in any particular sport. In some instances, the existing rules that govern sports at these different levels may conflict, particularly between international and national bodies as detailed in Table 5.2 above. As at mid-2023, many sporting associations had not developed their transgender policies in accordance with the IOC 2021 framework and still referred to the 2015 IOC guidelines including regulating testosterone levels (see Chapter 1 and Appendix A). The decision to include transwomen within female sport is becoming increasingly more contested among sports.

In September 2021, UK Sports including Sport England, Sport Scotland, Sport Northern Ireland, and Sport Wales released a revision of its earlier stance on transgender inclusion policies in non-elite sports. This latest version concluded that both competitive fairness and safety could not co-exist at the community level if transgender athletes were allowed to take part in female sports. However, it did conclude that fairness and safety for transmen athletes could be ensured in the male category in most sports. This report reiterated the conclusions of others, drawn from available biological evidence, that testosterone suppression was unlikely to create fairness between transwomen and natal women competitors.

In January 2022, the National Collegiate Athletic Association (NCAA) in North America released a new three phase policy about transgender participation which places the onus on each college sport to either develop their own policy, align their guidelines with their National or International body or follow the IOC framework. Phase one, applied in 2020, called for one year of testosterone suppression. Phase Two, beginning August 2022 to 2024, requires transwomen athletes to provide laboratory results providing evidence they meet sport-specific testosterone levels. These range between <10nmol/L (e.g., acrobatics, volleyball, golf), < 5nmol/L (e.g., rowing, tennis) and <2.5 nmol/L (water polo). Unfortunately, by our assessment, such an approach maintains the false assumption that regulating testosterone level evens the playing field and makes competition fair between natal males and females.

World Rugby has now been joined by World Aquatics in late 2022, and World Athletics and the Cycling Time Trials UK in 2023 with similar transgender bans in the women's category. These sports' policies now exclude transwomen who have experienced male puberty from competing in the female category at the elite level. The female category is reserved for those athletes who are born female. Athletes must never have gone through any part of male puberty and must maintain their serum testosterone levels below 2.5 nmol/L to be considered for the female category. A transman rider (born female) may ride in the female category, pending meeting the testosterone level regulation. Female-identifying or non-binary male riders must compete in the Open category in Cycling Time Trials events. World Aquatics and World Athletics are investigating an Open category, whereby any athlete regardless of the sex, legal gender, or gender identity could compete. We address such options in the next chapter.

It is encouraging too that major sports are starting to revisit their earlier participation policies, with insight from existing and emerging biological and sport science information. They are solving the practical issues surrounding gender identity in athletes. As we have stated before in the introduction, administrators and governing bodies, athletes, and the community all want the same thing – fair sport, safe sport, authentic sport for all-comers. The next chapter turns to possible solutions for the paradox of transgender inclusion in women's sport.

CHAPTER 6

Competition Integrity and Inclusion

As we have shown in previous chapters the biological evidence reveals a clear problem with fairness and safety for women when inclusion ignores biology. Contested arguments about whose rights prevail in the female category is at the heart of the transgender paradox. In an interview published in 2022, trans swimmer Lia Thomas declared "The very simple answer is that I'm not a man, I'm a woman, so I belong on the women's team." (Sports Illustrated, March 2022). How does sport address such biologically untrue claims yet enable trans athletes' legitimate opportunities in sport?

There is a desire amongst sporting codes to grow and broaden sporting opportunities for everyone, whether as a player, administrator, or coach, or across age, disability, or gender. They aim to engender respect to all who desire to play their sport at any level, within a socially safe environment, free from harassment, bigotry, or discrimination. To develop fair participation policies, sport governing bodies are grappling with gender ideology, human rights declarations, and biological science. These policies cannot run afoul of sex-discrimination or civil liberties legislation which casts both gender identity and sex as protected attributes. What solutions might there be for this daunting task?

Alternative Roles in Sport

While this text has thus far focused on the competing athlete, it would be remiss to not consider other sporting roles beyond the competitor. Inclusion could encompass a range of paid or volunteer positions within sport beside that of competitive athlete. Positions such as team manager, umpire, administrator, trainer, or coach can also provide the social connections and engagement for a marginalised person. Bodies such as Sport Australia, and Stonewall in the UK are urging sports to adopt an inclusive organizational culture, and to develop initiatives such as equality education, training modules for administrators, gender participation scorecards, and public declarations of sports' gender inclusion ethos.

We have seen over the past decade or so strident calls by trans supporters to redress social and health inequities of this marginalized minority because of unfair exclusion from society. Specifically, their calls have centred on the rights of transwomen athletes to join elite female competition yet with almost silence on reciprocal rights of transmen into male competition.

However, to open elite female sport to competitors based on their female identity and the fiction that 'transwomen are women' overly constrains potential opportunities, in our opinion. There are many other paths within sporting activity not reliant on either elite competition or being a competitor. Importantly, recreational physical activity already provides many avenues for healthy participation regardless of gender, age, culture, creed, or identity. Non-competitive physical activity such as hiking, surfing, cycling, swimming, gym work is readily available. Recreational, mixed sex leagues are common e.g., mixed touch rugby, mixed soccer, mixed netball, etc. All provide individuals with many options to engage in community sporting activities for social, physical, and mental well-being and their 'right to play sport'. We present below eight options for structuring sport that could achieve trans inclusion without compromising the integrity of the female category of sport.

Before we do so, there are some who argue that sport should be completely reformed to do away with binary sport. One radical approach is that of Erikainen, Vincent and Hopkins (2022), who propose sport should merit other criteria instead of physical performance and winning. To facilitate inclusion of all they suggest abandoning binary sex or gender structures and discarding any focus on competition and winning. Further, they posit that removing entrenched social and cultural hierarchies will positively impact the meaning and value of sport and enabling a refocus on the enjoyment of physical activity, teamwork, and personal growth in this 'new' form of sport. However, one could counter that this re-defined concept is not sport at all. Yes, sport is not for everyone, but it does include elements of pure enjoyment, participation for fun, collaboration, and personal growth, as does non-competitive recreational physical activity. Recreational activity is open to all, and available in many forms including yoga, dance, parkour, tai chi, trail walking, paddling, and swimming. Erikainen's vision in fact is not new: the 'Earth Games' movement of the 1970s embodied the ethos of 'non-competitive' games, in which participation, teamwork, and fun were goals, not winning.

Inclusion for all-comers in sport is a key objective, yet how can the inclusion of transwomen be achieved so that the sport remains safe, fair, and meaningful for everyone? Rather than 'shoehorning' trans-athletes into existing competition structures, we urge that innovative solutions could and should be sought. If sports wish to include all-comers in their code but maintain due consideration of rights, integrity, and meaningfulness, then sport policy makers need to identify models of competition that provide a balance between competing human rights for both natal and trans athletes while recognizing the truth of biological sex differences.

To this end we explore a range of options for competition that have either already been implemented by some sports to a greater or lesser extent, such as Options 5, 7, 8, 9 and 10, or are being actively considered as options, or are merely hypothetical proposals. For each option described below we have identified possible advantages and disadvantages. Whether an option is a solution for the transgender paradox will depend on the priority that a sport places on inclusion, fairness, or safety. Innovation in inclusive competition formats demands meaningful policy deliberations around sex, gender, and identity that also preserve the inherent good of sport to society and the individual. The first two options completely compromise the integrity of female sport and cannot be recommended.

Option 1. Self-declared Gender Identity

This is the current 'progressive' model favoured by transgender activists, yet it extinguishes the female category of sport. Sporting categories are decided by gender identity. Presumably this model would still regulate participant eligibility for other protected categories such as age, disability, or weight classes in combative sports.

The advantages of this option are that the rights of transgender athletes are affirmed by self-identity over biological sex. There are also some sports where safety and fairness are not compromised (for example, see Table 5.1 - horse-riding, bocce, social competitions). The clear disadvantage is that the rights of natal female athletes to a sex-based level playing field are abolished.

Option 2. Open Competition. No Categories

In this scenario there are no sex based binary categories. All and any athletes compete against each other regardless of gender/sex. This extinguishes the female category from most sports. There are some sports that have never had sex-based divisions, for example horse riding, motor sports, or shooting. Some ultra-endurance competitions, such as ultra-marathons and ultra-distance open water swimming, also fit into this category as females have a high capacity for such events. In swimming, the greater buoyancy and fat insulation of the female body appears to be a rare advantage in ultra-distance swimming sport. This is evidenced by the long-distance female swimmer Shelley Taylor-Smith who broke the world four-mile record, won the Manhattan Island Marathon swim five times (breaking the world record in 1995) and numerous other open swimming events.

This option promotes inclusivity and acceptance of gender diversity and would also simplify the administration of sporting competitions. However, fair, open competition for females is limited to a few forms of sport only. In most head-to-head events, female athletes would rarely win against biological males and transwomen who have a physical advantage. Furthermore, female athletes are likely to miss team selections as their performances would not merit selection. In addition, this option may create greater safety concerns for females competing, particularly for contact or combative sports.

Option 3. Mixed Sex Competitions

Transgender athletes already participate in a range of existing mixed sex sports competitions. For these, males and females form teams, with a specific allocation of each sex, according to rules of play and with consideration of player safety. In most sports, transwomen are deemed male members on the team in recognition of their male bodied advantage. Examples include mixed netball, tennis mixed doubles, korfball, and some of the new mixed events in Olympic Games. However, US Rowing's transgender policy effective from March 2023[1] specified that mixed crews for masters rowing adhere to a sex-based male:female ratio. Fifty percent of the crew must be those 'assigned as female at birth', and transwomen rowers are considered in the 50% male ratio. Yet without a hint of insight or irony, its women's category is deemed exclusively for athletes who identify as a woman at the start of the rowing season and/or those who are assigned as female at birth. This ruling shows double standards. Women's events become effectively 'mixed sex' events and female rowers lose out to male bodied rowers, but mixed sex events must adhere to strict natal sex criteria so there is 'fairness'.

This option has elements of inclusion, safety, and fairness for female athletes as opportunities are protected with sex-based quotas, and often rules regarding opponents in team sports being sex-matched. However, in mixed sex events as in the example of US Rowing, transwomen are classified as representing the male sex and counted in the male quota, not as their female identity. This protects fairness for natal males in a mixed event and ensures natal females can be included, yet such concerns are not afforded natal female rowers. It denies transwomen their self-identity, is deemed disrespectful and entirely unacceptable to some.

---

1. https://usrowing.org/documents/2022/11/28/Gender_Identity_Policy_021323.pdf

Option 4. Unisex Teams. Merit Based

Sports could devise unisex competitions, either team or individual, whereby the contest is based on a set of attributes, abilities, or skills pertinent to that sport. For example, golf and archery emphasise technical and/or tactical skills differently. Martinkova (2020) suggested that in order to balance male-female abilities, a unisex sport might be made more complex than its previous sex-based version. This could be accomplished by measuring a wider range of skills to determine the winner of a game (intercepts, passing effectiveness, evasion effectiveness, etc.) rather than a simple result such as number of goals scored.

A unisex sport would therefore result in a broader mixture of athletes of different sizes, shapes, abilities, and skills, thereby avoiding or mitigating sex specific advantages. Sailors (2016) also advocated that in developing such a model one would need to distinguish between individual and team sports; direct and indirect competition; contact and non-contact sports; and amateur and professional sports. Such as option very much depends on what abilities or skills are tested in the sport, and the merit so attached.

This option provides for inclusion, fairness and safety. It also enhances wider opportunities as players are chosen on broader skills and abilities which are the measured game outcomes. Furthermore, sex-based stereotypes may be challenged by demonstrating that both males and females can be equally skilled in a particular sport.

On the other hand there are a number of disadvantages. The sport specific nature of this option requires a significant amount of research, skill analysis and game development, given the different physical attributes of each sex. An algorithm to incorporate and weight the various attributes may not appear intuitive or be transparent to either players or spectators. A broader set of outcome attributes does not necessarily enhance player diversity. The criteria may result in selection being biased to one sex and not sport for all. In sport, female champions and world record holders are recognised in their own right, regardless of the men's records within the same event. However, in this new era, given the evidence of physical and performance superiority of an elite TW athlete, future sporting records set by TW are likely to set near-impossible benchmarks for natal female achievement. Will these times be considered authentic female records when set by TW athletes? Further, will aspirations of young female athletes be dashed when they compete against a TW athlete or when team selection is usurped by them? We do not know the views of the 21-year-old Samoan heritage NZ weightlifter who missed Olympic team selection for the 2020 Tokyo Games to a much older TW, but other coaches and athletes voiced their anonymous incredulity that this could have occurred.

Option 5. Handicapping

A variety of handicapping systems could be devised to balance unfair physical or social athletic advantages/disadvantages. For example, Foddy and Savulescu (2011) had suggested creating a hormonal level playing field by dividing sport, not along gender lines, but on testosterone levels with those above a specified level competing in the male or open category. Further, if this approach was adopted in sport, then it was suggested that women should be permitted to take a 'safe level' of exogenous testosterone to boost to whatever cutoff level. This is a radical departure from the current attempts to keep sports free from performance enhancing drugs and results to be on pure athletic merit. Such an approach erroneously assumes that male and females use circulating testosterone to the same extent, and that the effects of puberty for each sex is the same, despite very different hormonal interactions. We refer the reader back to Chapters 2 and 3 to understand the distinctly different physiology of males and females, and how circulating testosterone level does not define fairness in sport. Importantly, testosterone level varies with training load and does not correlate with sport performance, within sexes, within sports and within events.

Knox and colleagues (2019) expanded the concept of handicapping in sport, suggesting an algorithm to level the playing field based on social parameters such as gender identity and socioeconomic status, alongside physiological parameters such as size, haemoglobin levels, VO2 max, timing of gender transition, and testosterone levels. An algorithm would necessarily be tailored to specific sports, resulting in potentially multiple divisions within an event. Athletes could be placed into a division based on parameters such as height, weight, bone size, lung size, or wingspan in order to mitigate unfair physical and social parameters.

Another approach to handicapping could be using rule and equipment modifications to create fairness among athletes participating in the same event. For example, if competing in women's golf, and to account for their innate greater physical power, transwomen could hit off the male tee. Martinkova (2020) and Hämäläinen (2014) both suggested variations of ski jumping events with natal female athletes starting from a higher gate on a hill. Some have proposed that transwomen athletes wear weighted clothes, similar to racehorse handicaps, in order to compete in particular events, such as running races. Another approach is to start from different marks. For example, there is an annual, professional 120m footrace in Australia called the Stawell Gift in which runners from around the world vie for the prize money. They are handicapped on form and ability, starting off various marks.

This option provides elements of inclusion, safety, and fairness for female athletes. It also creates an opportunity for all athletes to compete at a high level.

On the other hand, rule and equipment modifications that permit males and females to compete together reinforces the view that without adjustments female athletes are inferior (for more problems with this approach see Pakaslahti, 2017). Designing a fair handicapping system is complex, requiring algorithms which are both intuitive and fair. Results of a race or event may be inconsistent and confusing to both spectators and athletes alike, when results are adjusted for the weighted physical attributes.

Even if new categories or algorithms were devised, males may still dominate these new categories. For example, handicapping based on testosterone level does not account for the performance advantage already inherent in the male physique, an enduring legacy of male puberty regardless of testosterone reduction in transwomen. Finally, handicap algorithms may also need to account for different training resources a male athlete is typically afforded during their development compared to females. Whether handicapping for all the possible biological and social parameters is feasible, arguably makes this option a non-starter.

Option 6. Pre- or Post-puberty Transgender Categories

Theoretically, this option has merit. Firstly, we have already established that pre-pubertal children can safely and fairly play on the same teams because biologically they are generally well-matched, and many sports have facilitated this in their junior age groups. So, whether a child feels they are trans or not, sports for children under the age of 12 years are typically 'gender-blind'. Such arrangements are permitted under the various iterations of sex discrimination, equal opportunity, human rights, and civil rights acts where pre-pubertal male and female children (defined as under 12s) compete together because biology indicates little sex-based advantages in childhood.

This is inclusive and fair for pre-pubertal boys identifying as girls (that is trans girls). It accommodates the very different physical growth and development outcomes for those who do not experience male puberty due to puberty blockers and female hormone therapy.

However, it could become problematic. For example, US Rowing allows youth under 19 years, and British Rowing allows youth under 16 years to row according to their gender identity regardless of birth sex. This ruling applies even though puberty will be underway for many if not most, and sex-difference in performance will favour males. In indoor rowing, the women's world record for 2k is 6:21.1. The male record for the 13-14 year age group is nearly 5s faster at 6:16.7 (Fair Play for Women, 28 December 2022).

Under this option, it may be possible for a boy who identifies as female and does not undergo male puberty to compete in the female category because puberty blockers means they fail to develop typical male physical and muscular attributes. As such they do not have an unfair physical advantage in sport over female competitors and would therefore be eligible to compete in the adult female category of a sport. World Aquatics has incorporated such a regulation within its 2022 transgender regulations.

While such a rule has appeal and affirms a child's gender identity the assumption that trans-questioning children will routinely undergo medical intervention to prevent puberty is ethically problematic. As discussed earlier in Chapter 2 in the section on transition treatment, the 'affirmation model of care' for trans children is under increasing scrutiny for lacking an evidence-base. Puberty blockers and cross hormone treatment are not without health risks for the child, including those who may later detransition and notwithstanding the child's capacity to give informed consent to such lifechanging treatment. For sport fairness, however, a case-by-case evaluation, requiring detailed medical information is required to verify a youth or adult athlete's claim to have not undergone male puberty. If such cases arise, the challenge for sports federations would be whether they have the expertise to regulate and the procedures to protect the athlete's right to medical privacy.

Option 7. Independent LGBT+ Competitions

Just as gay and lesbian communities have instituted their specific competitions, for example the Gay Games and the Pride Cup, transgender athletic community could develop their own stand-alone events, or be incorporated within such established events. In 2019, an historic, all-transgender ice hockey team (comprising both males and females) competed in a Friendship Tournament against an LGBTQ team, the Boston Pride. This type of event within the LGBT+ community provides a supportive and positive environment for athletes. The LGBT+ community could set their own rules re eligibility, such as no medical transition requirements.

On the other hand, such independent events or competition may reinforce 'separateness' from society, not inclusion. Such competitions may not provide sufficient challenge for trans athletes to reach their potential which may not be acceptable.

Option 8. Third Category: Non-binary

This option creates an additional category in sports competitions beyond male and female. It could be the non-binary/trans division. Those eligible for the latter category would include transgender, non-binary, gender fluid, or intersex athletes. This option is founded on the understanding that the inclusion of transwomen athletes cannot co-exist with the concept of fairness in a sport where strength, power and physique are significant advantages.

Such a solution for trans athletes is not without precedent. There are a growing number of examples across a range of sports. In 2017, Scottish Athletics created a third, non-binary category. If sufficient non-binary athletes enter, the event is run separately from the male and female events, otherwise the entrants run at the same time as the men's race. There are now over 200 running events around the world that offer inclusion via a non-binary gender identity classification, with five world marathons (London, New York, Chicago, Boston, Berlin) now offering a non-binary classification, the latest being the 2023 Boston Marathon. In December 2022, with much fanfare, USA Cycling held its first non-binary category cyclocross event in Hartford, Connecticut with four starters. The 2nd place getter Kristin Sundquist had planned to move across to the female division in 2023 but stricter UCI testosterone rules (2.5 nmol/L for 24 months) have delayed those plans.

In 2022, USA Powerlifting launched a new category 'MX' which provides competition space for all athletes in 14 weight classes no matter how they identify. This mirrors those of the LGBT Powerlifting Union and 2020 Gay Games. There are also more non-binary options in endurance sports like cycling, Cyclocross, distance running, and multi-event sports such as triathlon. For example, The Jedburgh Ultramarathon race includes a non-binary category, now on an equal footing with the women's and men's category.

Some sports such as World Boxing, which has banned fighting between males and females regardless of gender identity, are currently planning to create a specific category for transgender fighters. The sex-based ban is grounded on a primary concern for the safety of the athletes. Several national boxing associations and Mixed Martial Arts (MMA) are now also following suit. MMA are considering developing a points system similar to that used in paralympic sport to distinguish between the transitioning stage of the athletes – either pre puberty, post puberty, and the duration of medical transitioning.

This initiative is a fair and safe solution for natal females, upholding their right to their biological sex category. It offers a supportive and positive environment for both natal females and transgender athletes. At the same time there is increased visibility and representation for the transgender community in sports. Thus, it validates the identity of all non-binary, gender fluid and trans athletes.

The non-binary category could be seen as empowering, providing an opportunity to compete in a category true to one's identity, rather than not to compete at all as it does not force non-binary athletes to compete in the male or female divisions. Transmen are also accommodated; hitherto they are often ignored in the current debate. Finally, the safety of all athletes is ensured, particularly in combative and grappling, and contact sports.

Nonetheless, this option could stigmatize, with some trans athletes seeing a third category as denying their legitimacy as a person. Some transwomen claim such exclusion from the female category is a denial of their identity as a women. For example, Kate Weatherly a trans New Zealand Downhill Mountain in 2019 stated "My thing is, I'm not gender neutral, I'm a girl. The whole idea of a third category [besides female, male] invalidates my sense of identity". The non-binary label may offend those who identify as a transwoman or transman.

The limited number of competitors able to participate in the trans/non-binary categories may make the competition less attractive but on the positive side, in a smaller field there is a greater chance of winning. Potentially, the overall prize pool becomes sub-divided into three rather that two, which provides more opportunities for male-bodied athletes to prizes - two prize pools for male bodied athletes (non-binary/transwomen, and natal male), and one prize pool for natal female athletes. In addition, this model may limit the opportunity for transgender athletes to compete against the best at the highest level in their sport, potentially hindering their athletic development and progress.

Finally, this category may be open to fraud. Some males may choose to compete in such events because there is a greater chance to win prize money due to the lower numbers of competitors. The rules of eligibility may be 'gamed'.

Option 9. Sub-classification System

The example of paralympic sport could be a model going forward for authentic transgender athlete inclusion. At the heart of the para sport movement are the twin factors of athlete rights and fairness in the competitions, both elements at the core of the current inclusion paradox. Paralympic sport has developed a sophisticated, within-disability classification system to provide competitive fairness for those whose disabilities affect competitive capability and to cater for low numbers of competitors in any disability category. It is universally acknowledged that, as with disability sport in earlier years, currently the numbers of transgender people in sport are also tiny which is therefore an impediment to opportunities for competition. Para sports have undertaken serious, innovative effort to champion diversity and inclusion. By creating sport on their own terms there has been a surge in the numbers of new competitors into a wide variety of sports. In some major events such as the Commonwealth Games, trials are being held to integrate para events into the main program rather than as a separate major sporting competition.

Other classification systems in sport have also pointed to how safety and fairness are maximized for the competitors. These are weight categories such as in boxing, wrestling, and weightlifting as well as age categories for children's or masters' sports. In the teenage years, New Zealand youth rugby categorises players by physique, such as height and weight rather than age to accommodate different pubertal growth rates among boys of different ethnic heritages. Age-banding and points systems are effective in Masters' competitions to include increasing numbers of older athletes into their 90s. A range of ages may compete in the same event (this model accommodates small numbers within an age group) but the track times, distance thrown, or height jumped are compared within the participant's age band to determine placings and records. While these various classification systems are not perfect, they demonstrate the serious effort applied by sporting bodies over the years to create new competitive opportunities that are fair for athletes with disabilites. Could the transgender sub-classification events be integrated within mainstream sports competition?

There are some clear advantages. Competitions that integrate transgender athletes within their own division, as distinct from a third non-binary category, would not compromise fairness and safety for female athletes. Trans athletes would achieve recognition without usurping female achievements. Trans athletes could also be included as a sub-classification within a representative/national team.

There are also disadvantages similar to those for a non-binary, third category. For example, sub-classification may not be considered an affirmation of identity for transwomen athletes. It is possible that the very small numbers in many sports may still make it unviable for administrators to schedule a separate event within a main program for transgender athletes. Very small fields of competitors may result in mediocre performances through lack of competitive pressure. Finally, like the previous option prize monies become diluted for women, as three prize pools are created – two for male bodied athletes (transwomen, and male), one for natal female athletes.

Option 10. Two Categories Only. Female and Open

This option is a pared back version of Option 7. It merely relabels the male category as open and is a division for all comers regardless of sex or gender identity if they so choose - any natal male, natal female, transwoman, transman, non-binary, or other gender identity. The category is defined neither by gender identity nor biological sex. Under this regime, the female category is protected as a discrete sex-based division, exclusively for competitors born female. Transwomen athletes would be excluded from competing in the female category. The case for females who identify as other than female (transmen, or non-binary for example) and who are not taking any male hormones are eligible female competitors. USA athletes Quinn, an Olympic soccer player and Nikki Hiltz a 1500m runner are two such cases.[2] (refer to Appendix B).

This option is now being implemented from 2023 by British Triathlon. The female category is only for those who are female at birth, with all trans athletes from 12 years of age being restricted to the Open category. World Aquatics is also examining the potential for an Open category in which any athlete would be able to compete regardless of their sex, gender, or gender identity. According to latest 2022 World Aquatics regulations, transwomen can only compete in the female category if they had transitioned before puberty, with testosterone levels maintained below 2.5 nmol/L (See

---

[2]. A section on non-binary and transmen athletes is included in Appendix B on the book's website. The link to access additional online resources is provided at: https://doi.org/10.18848/978-1-957792-73-6/CGP

Appendix A). This option therefore prioritises fairness and safety for natal females. Other advantages are that trans athletes compete within a 'mainstream' category, not as a 'fringe' competitor in their separate minor division and the female only category ensures opportunities for women to participate are retained and achievements are rightfully recognized.

On the contrary, there is a view among trans advocates that having a single 'Open' category for all except female swimmers, does not solve the problem of fairness to trans athletes. In an Open division, transwomen, who may be on hormone suppressants and whose physical capacities are lessened from their male potential, would be competing against their unmedicated 'brothers' and may not meet the required performance standards to progress in some meets. Additionally, for transmen it is highly improbable that their performance standard would match their biological male peers (cis or trans) even with testosterone supplementation. The changes wrought by testosterone on their female biology does not match the changes experienced by male puberty. One could argue that under this two-category option transgender athletes will become invisible in sport. Potentially, trans athletes could not achieve podium finishes or make a career of sport because of little success despite motivation, training, and dedication (the same negative consequence of transwomen in female sport).

Summing Up

In this chapter we have addressed whether there are solutions to fair and safe inclusion of transgender athletes. In doing so we first pointed to many other roles within sport, beside that of the competing athlete, through which transgender people may be meaningfully involved. We also addressed the opportunities that are available through recreational sport. Each of these roles and opportunities enables social engagement and participation within the sporting landscape. Yet the demands by transwomen to participate in women's sport is a paradox that must be reconciled.

To that end, we have assembled ten competition format options, each having been promoted in either the research literature or social media. Some are already established practice, others merely proposed by sporting bodies. Of those suggested, the two options that emerge from within sex-based categories, and with support among female athletes involve the creation of an open category, either as a third non-binary/trans category purely for non-binary/trans athletes (Option 8) or including all transwomen athletes within the natal male category (Option 10). While some of the other options may be more attractive to the trans community (Option 1 in particular), these prioritise the rights of a very small number of trans athletes over every female athlete and thereby perpetuates unfairness and safety issues. A level playing field no longer exists within many transgender inclusion policies. It is now time that sports policy takes account of the biological evidence as relevant to their sport and devise more nuanced solutions to the transgender paradox in women's sport.

CONCLUSION

Closing the Paradox Argument

In this final chapter we return to the transgender paradox – that the female category is no longer what it is described as but is dual sex. The recent transgender inclusion policies have recklessly opened the female category of sport to trans identifying biological males, to the detriment of biological females for whom that category was always designed. Female athletes' concerns have been largely ignored and they are being compelled under these 'progressive rules' by sporting bodies to welcome male-bodied athletes into their competitions.

However, the biological evidence presented in this text clearly shows why such a paradox is untenable. The advancement of women's sport and recognition of its unique character is centred in the biology of the sexes and must remain so. Lobbying by trans activists has led to sport inclusion policies which at their core, embrace gender identity to be a person's truthful persona, and that it is an athlete's human right to have their self-declared gender identity validated through sport.

In this text the biological evidence clearly dispels gender identity as a valid criterion for grouping sport categories. We showed that the idea that hormonal adjustments in transwomen ensure fairness and safety for natal females in sport is a myth. Biological science informs us that the beliefs that 'transwomen are women', that gender transition alters someone's biological sex, that transition removes physical performance differences are not tenable.

Sporting bodies are tasked with the promotion and administration of sport for all comers, as they play an important role in society, empowering participants and promoting health and social benefits at both the individual and societal level. However, the advent of specific inclusion policies for gender diverse and transgender people, is likely to hamper the advances female sport has made over the years.

Our review of sports transgender guidelines shows that the testosterone regulations are increasingly variable. Testosterone levels are set at 10, 5 or 2.5 nmol/L, and for minimum durations from 12 to 24 to 36+ months. Such variations illustrate how arbitrary these designated levels are and that ever-reduced testosterone rules for otherwise healthy male bodies cannot be the answer.

We wrote this text to provide the biological arguments to counter the prevailing gender ideology beliefs that have captured sport policy development. We urge a spirit of scientific openness and respect for concerns of all who want to play sport at any level. All seek a socially safe environment, one that is free from harassment. However, the integrity of female competition should not, indeed cannot, be abandoned to satisfy the wants of a trans biological male.

Here are seven key messages that capture the themes in this biological exposé.

Key Message 1
The category of women's sport must be protected

Over the past 100 years or so, the sports industry has gradually improved gender equality. The pioneering women athletes who developed their own competitions, or spin-offs from male sports have provided opportunities for girls and women through a separate 'protected' sports category. For the first time in the history of the Olympics, equal numbers of male and female athletes and near equal number of events were achieved at the 2020 Tokyo Games.

As females comprise 50 percent of the general population their right to fair and safe sporting opportunities should be undoubted. This is predicated on the fairness for girls and women to play against athletes of their own 'biological type' i.e., females. From adolescence and beyond, male bodies become on average physically bigger, stronger, faster, and more powerful – these physical characteristics enable superior sporting performances compared to age-matched females. Having females compete head-to-head against males in the same event is neither fair nor safe, nor does it promote the interests of women's participation.

The IOC and national sport governing bodies have all developed clear gender equality goals and have resourced programs to redress the hitherto imbalance in funding, coaching, facilities, and career opportunities for female athletes. Girls and women wanting to play sport against their biological kind on a level playing field is not a show of disrespect to anyone, it's merely standing up for equity.

We uphold that women's sport provides a social good for its participants. Accordingly, sporting bodies must take positive steps to safeguard the growth and prosperity of female sport. They must assure that the human rights of their female participants are also protected, and that competition maximises fairness and safety to females. A sports competition without integrity or authenticity is meaningless to society, and if the gender participation policies go uncorrected, inevitably girls and women will be the big losers (Coleman, 2017). At present, girls and women are being discriminated against, they are being disrespected, and their needs are being ignored. It appears that in advocating for special treatment of male 'wants' over female 'needs' in sport the trans movement is supporting a new form of sexual discrimination.

Key Message 2
Regulating testosterone levels is a distraction

The regulation of current serum testosterone levels has become the go-to solution for achieving "fairness" in female sports. Ever lower levels of testosterone at 10 nmol/L over 12 months (IOC 2015), to 5 nmol/L (US Swimming 2021) or 2.5 nmol/L over 36 months (World Aquatics 2022) or 24 months (UCI, 2023) have been set to supposedly mitigate or reverse the effects of male physical development in puberty. Despite this, biological evidence has shown an unbalanced effect. Decreasing testosterone levels post puberty does not reverse the physical changes in the body to its pre-pubertal state. It is true that lowered testosterone concentration, even to within the female range, does affect the male physiology by reducing muscle bulk, muscle strength, and haemoglobin levels but there is little evidence that this results in a reduction corresponding to female level performances.

The main issue is that from the early weeks of gestation the male physiology is exposed to life-long testosterone levels that greatly exceed female levels. Puberty then supercharges the release of testosterone, and the boy becomes a sexually mature adult. The long-term effects of male puberty are not reversible, and evidence thus far shows that athletic capabilities developed during puberty persist beyond at least three years of cross hormone therapy. The physical advantages therefore make mixed sex competition in most sports unfair and unsafe.

Female biology is uniquely designed for pregnancy, birth, and breastfeeding driven by cyclic female hormones such as estrogen and progesterone. To reach the top, athletic females adapt training volumes, diet and recovery not only around competition schedules but also to account for their unique physiological cycles in menstruation, and for some post-partum, and breastfeeding. These constraints are never experienced by male athletes. That is why we uphold that sport among 'biological equals' does not mean merely 'equal' testosterone levels.

Key Message 3
Fairness and safety cannot co-exist with transgender inclusion

Principle 5 of the 2021 IOC framework urges sports to make 'no presumption of advantage' in relation to transwomen athletes in female sports. In contradiction of that position, we have presented unequivocal biological evidence that instead advises great caution, and setting new policy directions in ignorance of existing, peer-reviewed evidence (yes, it is incomplete) would be unwise at best, and negligent at worst.

We presented the current biological evidence of sex-based female disadvantage; we outlined its importance to sport policies; presented a perspective on whether fairness and safety can co-exist with inclusion; and catalogued alternate competition options congruent with the goal of protecting women's sports.

We concluded that the paradox in women's sport arose from transgender policies promulgating unfounded beliefs. These are that gender identity is the true self; that it is a simple, fair concept in relation to sport; that the concept of sex is fluid, complex and contested by science; that those who identify as women have no advantage over natal women; that rules to bar transwomen are gender discriminatory; and that sex-divisions in sport are outdated, serving no purpose.

Sport needs to find other options to accommodate and grow the transgender participant base. There is merit in sports finding solutions suited to their distinct situation. Even at community level, natal females may feel affronted by trans inclusion. Sports do have a duty of care to ensure the physical safety of females against a stronger, more powerful male physique. Analysing a sport's placement within the 'hierarchy of contact' appears a useful approach.

However, sports ought to ask the fundamental questions: 'Why do we have a female category of sport?', and 'What adverse consequence could occur for our female players from this fundamental change to female category eligibility?'. Weak policy making has resulted from incurious administrators, capitulating to the vested interests of the transgender movement. Instead, evidence should first be shown to support any mooted change in rules by those seeking the change.

> Key Message 4
> Whose voice is heard? Who is being silenced?
> Who is at the table?

Research needs to explore the perspectives of all those affected by policy shifts, not only the select group for whom a change is advocated. All stakeholders, all voices, without prejudgement, have a right to be represented at the policy table. When the integrity of competitions might be compromised by a policy shift, one could expect sporting bodies to be especially careful in their deliberations. Our research has led us to the conclusion that this paradox in women's sport arose because too many at the decision table were convinced this change was the right thing to do and accepted at face value the sociological 'evidence' from trans advocate organizations to the exclusion of biological science.

In trying to understand the process by which sporting bodies, including the IOC, arrived at the acceptance of the notion of gender identity, and transwomen's right to play women's sport, we were struck by the opaqueness of the process. The published documentation we could access did not reveal from whom the input was sought, nor which submissions were used or ignored.

For example, the documented consultation process undertaken by Sport Australia and Australian Human Rights Commission with sporting bodies ahead of their 2019 guidelines provided minimal information about the stakeholders involved. Only a generic description of participant groups was published, such as sports administrators, government and non-government officials, medicos, academics, and athletes. There was no information about what effort if any was made to consult with the group most affected by new guidelines, natal female athletes. Few female athletes appeared to be aware, consulted or surveyed, nor were they at the discussion table when deliberations crucial to their sport were being held. These deliberations recast the fundamental basis of women's sport in Australia from being for athletes of the female sex to being for those whose gender identity is female; natal females were sidelined. Sport Australia and the peak sporting bodies do not appear to have played their key role advocating the interests of female athletes.

Unfortunately, the recent 2021 IOC update policy on transgender participation is similarly vague. There is no accompanying list of consultations sought, submissions received, nor indication of who attended the meetings and discussions beyond the composition of its gender panel. We do not know the answers to the question - Who was the advocate standing up for female sport? Who was representing biological science evidence? Who was presenting a transgender point of view? Who provided medical input?

Nevertheless, two trans advocacy groups have had a major influence on the transgender policy deliberations, and continue to do so - ACON in Australia, and Stonewall in the UK. These are not sports organizations. They represent the wider interests of the LGBT+ community. As we have revealed in Chapter 2, transgender people are currently a tiny proportion of the overall athletic population, yet these groups have exerted completely disproportionate influence on sport inclusion policies in their respective countries. Such groups argued that because this was about transgender and gender diverse athletes' inclusion, only the views of transgender athletes are relevant. The result is the transgender paradox in women's sport, a warped result devoid of sensible, workable, or fair solutions. Claims of wide consultation cannot be verified. Why weren't female voices heard?

In the lead up to the IOC's 2021 guidance, it was reported by Tucker that he and other specialist exercise physiologists were approached to provide up to date biological data such as that of Pike, Hilton and Howe (2021) but this submission is not listed. The IOC panel appeared to pay little heed to the existing published, unequivocal, biological and sport science evidence detailing unfair competition between the sexes and concluded that 'more evidence is needed' to decide whether transwomen have a 'disproportionate advantage' in women's sport. It declared that transwomen athletes must first be included in female sports (the 'no advantage' principle) and only excluded if specific evidence shows advantage for that sport or event. It is difficult to fathom the basis for that principle. Again, why were only some voices heard and only some types of expertise sought? Who had a seat at the table?

The key outcome of trans inclusion sport policies is to shift the onus solely onto the female category to be the solution for the transgender problem. As we have explained, there is no issue or apparent clamour for the inclusion of transmen into male sports (see key message 5 below). It is female sport that was expected to 'roll over' and accept an unfair solution. However, in the last few years, increasingly brave female athletes are standing up to transgender incursions into female sport. Their voices of dissent are growing and becoming more resolute. They are demanding a seat at the policy table too, despite being attacked for their bravery in standing up for women athletes.

In early April 2022, the controversy surrounding UK trans rider Emily Bridges (See Chapter 4), prompted many current and former elite riders to sign an open letter to British Cycling to request International Cycling (UCI) to rescind its transgender inclusion policy and support female cycling. For the first time, female riders threatened to boycott UK races because of the unfairness and safety concerns. British Cycling has suspended its inclusion policy pending review, ensuring for the time being that the female category is for natal females only.

In late April 2022, Australian Tokyo Olympic Gold medallists Emma McKeon, Emily Seebohm, and former champion Dawn Fraser spoke publicly against the unfairness of male-bodied athletes being included in female swimming tournaments, following the winning exploits of Lia Thomas in the US NCAA championships. Organisations have recently emerged to advocate for sustaining the meaning of biological sex in sport, the right to sex-segregated sports, and single-sex spaces, programs, and benefits, such as Save Women's Sport Australasia, Fair Play for Women (UK), Women's Sport Foundation (USA), Sex Matters (UK) and WomenSport International. Despite being labelled 'anti-trans hate groups' these groups maintain a clear focus on sex-based female rights.

Key Message 5
Male sport is completely untouched by these policies

The transgender guidelines will not hurt existing male sports or opportunities one iota. It is clear in the guidelines, that the regulation of the participation of transmen athletes is relatively relaxed. If a transitioning transman athlete does not begin androgenizing hormone treatment, they are still eligible to participate in the female category (e.g., US college swimmer Iszac Henig) as their physiology is female. If they choose to begin testosterone supplementation, then they are no longer allowed into the female category but can enter the male divisions pending the lodging of a therapeutic exemption certificate.

For transmen, cross hormone therapy in transition raises testosterone serum levels to perhaps the lower range of typical male levels, at best. The female physique becomes more masculinized and secondary sex characteristics emerge and muscle bulk and strength are gained over their female counterparts. Nonetheless, they can never match the physical ability or strength of their natal male counterparts. Transmen who compete as men are not a threat to male athletic achievement nor sporting records, rewards, and sponsorships, nor podium finishes. We posit that if male competitions and male athletes were adversely affected by new rules (transgender or not), as now for natal females in their category, then a much more hesitant or sceptical stance would be taken.

Key Message 6
Transgender athletes' rights to play sport are not denied

No person is being denied their right to play sport should the current transgender rules be rescinded, and eligibility merely restores the basic right of women to their own protected, sex-based competition. Such revisions are only barring male-bodied athletes from this female protected category. To foster transgender athlete participation in sport requires creative thought around alternative solutions. To that end we summarized a range of options in the previous chapter, many of which have previously been suggested in the literature or are already in place in some sports. To solve the transgender paradox, sports federations would be better placed to dedicate their time and effort to instigate new competition models.

Unlike transwomen athletes who may choose their sport category, such as women's, open, or third categories, women displaced from their own female sport category have no other competition to join. It is worth pointing out that only males can be transwomen and, by rights it is for males to embrace their 'gender diverse brothers' and solve their sport inclusion demands. In reverse, only females can be transmen. It is for females to accept their 'gender diverse sisters' and find workable solutions. This has already happened with lesbian (e.g., Martina Navratilova, tennis), non-binary female athletes (e.g., Quinn, US Olympic soccer player) and transmen (e.g., Iszac Henig, US College swimmer) participation.

The existing 'simple' solution of shoehorning a new type of athlete within the female category is neither fair, nor safe, nor protective of the integrity of women's sport. Retaining sex-based competition is crucially important for women's sporting opportunities and achievements to prosper. We assert that women's sport should not be martyred on the altar of inclusion and women should not have to give up their rights in sport for the opposing rights of a natal male.

Key Message 7
Research: New Questions

In unravelling the complexities around gender identity, most published studies in the field, including the IOC in its 2021 framework (Principles 6 and 10), call for more research. We support this call. It is crucial that the right questions are asked, and correct methods applied. This means that biological research should not be discounted but neither does it mean that social-psychological approaches should be ignored. However, in the parlance of research methodologies, mixed methods could be valuable to understanding, a method combining both quantitative-biological and qualitative-social approaches.

Research interest in gender diverse populations in sport is growing. Many studies investigate the psycho-social aspects of trans youth and adults' lives, the barriers to their participation in sport and physical education, social justice, and human rights issues. Biological studies comparing male-female differences in sports performance and the after-effects of transition are adding new information. New questions are being asked about whether the latest testosterone level of 2.5 nmol/L in several sports is even feasible for an otherwise healthy male athlete. Medical experimentation in the name of inclusion in sport must be approached with great caution. Adverse side effects of testosterone withdrawal, such as early onset osteoporosis are reported in the literature. Whether socially or biologically focussed, gender research is difficult because of the low prevalence of transgender individuals in the community, cited to range from 0.5 to 1.3% for self-reported gender dysphoria in children, adolescents and adults, and privacy concerns in recruiting participants for long term studies.

There is a need for longitudinal studies, to track changes in trans athletes as they undergo transition hormonal therapy and maintain sex-specific hormone profiles. There is a need to understand how transitioning prior to the onset of puberty, if permissible by local law, affects the male physiology. Much of the discussion about unfairness arises around cases in which the male athlete transitions post puberty, with the assumption that transitioning pre-puberty removes any residual advantage. This is an untested hypothesis. Further, we need information on whether early, pre-pubertal transitioning changes the balance between inclusion and fairness or safety.

Under the 2021 IOC transgender and sport guidelines, the requirement is now that sports can only justify transwomen bans by conducting their own research within those specific events. On the surface this appears to be a laudable plea to sports, but it ignores serious practical realities. In agreement with Ross Tucker's view, we dispute whether individual sports federations even have the resources or competency for this specialist research task. Perplexingly, Tucker reported that although unequivocal, biological evidence already exists to inform policy, the IOC did not use the evidence provided, to inform its latest 2021 policy.

Finally, in this 'progressive' inclusion era, it will be paramount for sports to monitor wider statistics at the individual and the systems level in female sports to reveal consequences, both positive and unintended. Base data such as participant numbers; the injury tally and causes; individual performance records; trans athlete representation at state and national level; and changes in sponsorship of women's sports, among others should be collected and reported. Although these data are essential, and complementary to further bio-physiology studies, we fear that such data collection and reporting compliance may be an untenable diversion of scarce resources.

Despite the celebrated examples in media stories, from which the cases in Appendix B are drawn, trans athletes' privacy is embedded in each of transgender policy statements in Australia and overseas and there is no objective way of tracking the growth or dropout of transgender athletes in sport. Privacy will likely make it illegal to use case-data originally collected for eligibility applications unless explicit, informed consent is given for wider, general research purposes Therefore, it is likely that key, reliable evidence necessary to either confirm the worth of a new sports policy or to rescind it will not be forthcoming.

In conclusion...a paradox is a proposition that appears sound in its reasoning (the gender identity position) but that leads to a logically unacceptable or self-contradictory conclusion (that males may compete against females, with opposing group rights). In closing the paradox argument, we ask again, should inclusion in sporting categories based on biological sex or gender identity, and for women's sport particularly which should be upheld to ensure fairness and safety? We conclude that for the great majority of sports, the clearest possible answer is in biological science – from puberty onwards, women's sport is for those whose sex at birth is female.

GLOSSARY

There are many sources that provide definitions of contemporary gender terminology. The list below is of the key terms used in this textbook. For more comprehensive guides to the diverse language and terminology in the gender literature one could consult, for example:

- Pride in Sport https://www.prideinsport.com.au/terminology/
- Healthline (2019). Provides 64 terms that describe gender identity and expression, https://www.healthline.com/health/different-genders
- American Psychological Association. (2015). Guidelines for Psychological Practice with Transgender and Gender Nonconforming People. American Psychologist, 70(9), 832-864. https://doi.org/10.1037/a0039906
- New Zealand Human Rights Commission Transgender Inquiry (2008). Resources/ Terminology https://www.hrc.co.nz/our-work/sexual-orientation-and-gender-identity/inquiry-discrimination-experienced-transgender-people/

Cis gender (Gender normative): cis gender man (cis man, cis male) or cis gender woman (cis woman, cis female) is one whose perceived gender identity conforms with the culturally determined gender roles for one's birth sex. Gender-critical scholars argue 'cis' to be a redundant prefix, because the noun man or woman defines the gender conforming person. In this text we use the adjective 'natal' instead of 'cis' to make it clear we are describing the biological/birth sex of the person, regardless of their gender identity or sexual orientation.

Discrimination: There are two usages referring to

1. A point of distinction based on criteria or characteristics that differentiate between people, or
2. A negative, moral connotation as in depriving people of various possibilities and benefits.

DSD (differences in sex development, intersex). A rare, genetic condition by which an individual inherits both male and female gonadal tissue, despite external genitalia at birth appearing normal, though genitalia may be ambiguous. Such individuals' gender is taken according to their physical appearance at birth. In otherwise identified females, testosterone is released from male gonads at puberty, resulting in androgenized physique characteristics (stature, muscular body shape, facial hair, etc.). In otherwise identified males, estrogen/progesterone is released from female gonads at puberty and ovulation and menses, and some feminization of physique may occur. In sport, athletes with DSDs are overrepresented in middle distance, female track events.

Equality: Equivalent treatment or parity measures to ensure equal opportunity.

Equity: The concept of fair, just treatment or measures to ensure parity or fair play such as funding and resources to mitigate economic or social disadvantages. Does the advantage provide all-purpose benefit, such as testosterone, compared to short stature (advantage in gymnastics but not basketball)?

Fairness (sport/competition): All athletes start from roughly the same starting point. No unfair advantage physically (hence sex categories, weight divisions, age division, rules around sporting technology, the rules of play agreed by participants). The genetic lottery which confers natural advantages on athletes are considered as tolerable unfairness in sport. At elite level, athletes become increasingly similar with respect to physique or abilities that match success for that sport – s self-selection into sports.

Female / Male: F – of or denoting the sex that can produce large gametes (ova) and designated as XX genetically. M – of or denoting the sex that can produce small gametes (sperm) and designated XY genetically (see also Sex).

Female sport: These are interchangeable labels denoting the sport category or competition set aside for athletes of the female sex. Distinct from the male category, mixed-sex sports, or open competitions.

Gay: male homosexual; same sex attraction to males.

Gender-critical. An adjective used to describe one who questions the tenets of gender ideology and who see biological sex as the fundamental basis of female oppression. Gender-critical scholars and commentators are often labeled by transgender activists as transphobic, bigoted, TERFs (see below), cis-supremacists, and inciting hatred through speech

Gender dysphoria (previously trans sexual, or gender identity disorder;). A medical diagnosis for persistent, profound, intense discomfort with one's gender identity (as manifested by typical dress, mannerisms, and social expression of preferred gender)

and the physical traits of their sex. Trans advocates are calling for the term gender incongruence to be used (as in the upcoming revision, ICD-11) as to de-medicalize the condition.

Gender identity: Gender is the social or cultural trait associated with the cultural norms of being masculine and feminine. Gender identity is the deeply felt, inner concept of self as a boy, a man, or male; or a girl, a woman, or female; or an alternative gender (e.g., genderqueer, gender nonconforming, gender neutral, non-binary). This conviction may or may not correspond to a person's sex at birth or to a person's physical sex characteristics. People are free to define their own gender identity, and there are a range of terms used in the gender spectrum. Being internal gender identity may not necessarily be obvious to others unless the person 'comes out'.

Gender non-conforming (also gender creative): describes persons who do not follow assumed societal male or female gender roles or typical expression or behaviors. Non-binary, or gender-neutral people have no preferred male or female gender identity. Fluid gender people have changing gender identity on any day.

Genderqueer: people who do not conform to traditional gender norms and express a non-standard gender identity. Some may not change their physical appearance or cross dress, but identify as genderqueer, gender neutral or androgynous.

Inclusion (in sport): the principle that sport should facilitate participation by all comers, derived from a 'human right' to play sport, irrespective of sex, gender, age, culture, or religious belief.

Lesbian: female homosexual; same sex attraction to the female sex.

Man: Adult male human being, the meaning based in biological reality. Now redefined within gender ideology as an adult who lives and identifies as a male even though they have been born as a different sex.

Natal female / natal male: Refers to the individual's biological birth sex, being female XX or male XY.

Sex: The biological categorization into male or female. Sex is determined at fertilization and for the vast majority of births may be confirmed anatomically either during pre-natal ultrasound investigation or at birth based on the external genitalia (primary sex characteristics). Sex is imbued in all aspects of cellular function and physiology from 'womb to tomb'. While there are several indicators of biological sex, including sex chromosomes, gonads, internal reproductive organs, and external genitalia, the key distinction between the sexes are the reproductive gametes produced from the gonads, either ovum (female) or sperm (male). (Also see, Female/Male; Intersex; Natal female/Natal male).

Sex-divided Sport: Traditionally sport competitions are divided according to the biological (natal) sex of the athlete. Women's sport is a protected category for athletes of the female sex. Adolescent and mature females are biologically and physiologically different to their male counterparts and cannot match the physical prowess of age-matched, same-sized males (Hilton & Lundeberg, 2021; Pike, Hilton and Howe, 2021). The female division in sport is to ensure females are competitive against members of their same sex group.

Testosterone: The androgenizing hormone responsible for building bodily tissues. In males it is produced by testes, in females trace amounts are released from the ovaries. Released in large amounts during puberty, testosterone causes the development of male secondary sex characteristics, bodily and facial hair, voice, as well as muscle bulk and physique, and sexual maturity. Athletes with the genetic condition 46XY 5-ARD DSD, are often designated female at birth because their external genitalia are visibly more female although they are biologically male. At puberty however, testosterone is released from inherited testicular tissue causing physical growth changes as expected for males. These biological males with DSD excel in middle distance track events The IAAF has stated, "To the best of our knowledge, there is no other genetic or biological trait encountered in female athletics that confers such a huge performance advantage" (Explanatory notes IAAF eligibility regulations for the female classification. 2018. https://www.documentcloud.org/documents/4449931-Explanatory-Notes-IAAF-Eligibility-Regulations.html)

Transgender (trans) (Adjective): People born with typical male of female anatomies but feel as if they have been born into the wrong body. Trans is an umbrella term that incorporates diversity of felt gender identities which are not matched with one's biological sex. Trans also includes non-binary or non-identifying persons who do not identity as either gender.

Transwoman / trans identifying male / MtF / XY Female: Male to female gender transition; a natal male who identifies as a female. Throughout we use the compound noun 'transwoman' to signify this is a subtype of person who identifies as transgender. We do not agree with the alternate label 'trans woman' whereby the addition of an adjective before the noun implies a type of woman. This latter descriptor is biologically illogical, though it is the form favored by trans advocatess and trans scholars.

Transman / trans identifying female / FtM / XX Male: Female to male gender transition; a natal female who identifies as male. See the description in transwoman, above, for the reason we use the compound noun transman, as a subtype of person rather than a subtype of man.

Transphobia: Transphobia refers to a range of negative stereotypes, feelings or behaviors towards anyone who is transgender or gender diverse, which often leads to prejudice or discriminatory actions or abuse; an irrational fear or anxiety of transgender individuals. Phobias are characterized by emotions of fear, terror, anxiety, fright. This pejorative label is the most used to refer to anyone who raise concerns or question the basic tenets of transgender ideology. See also Gender-critical.

Trans hesitant / Trans negative: Refer to those showing doubt, caution, or uncertainty perceptions about trans people. This label is more nuanced and allows that a questioning stance is not necessarily 'phobic.'

Transitioning: Steps taken by trans people to live in their felt gender identity. This includes dress and lifestyle, use of preferred pronouns, alternation of gender on civil identity documents (birth certificate, passport, drivers' license etc. depending on the laws of the country), and often medical treatment. Medical treatment typically involves hormone therapy (puberty blockers in adolescents, cross sex hormone therapy, and hormone suppression) and may include gender surgery (to remove gonads (hormone suppression) or genital surgery to mimic their felt identity). Transitioning is not a life phase, it is lifelong treatment, unless the person decides to detransition).

TERF (Acronym). Trans Exclusive Radical Feminists. A derogatory label applied to scholars who espouse arguments counter to those of transgender advocates' activism, particularly in the context of infringing female rights and protections afforded by existing sex discrimination laws.

Woman: Adult female human being, the meaning based in biological reality. With the advent of gender identity ideology, the noun 'woman' has been redefined thus, an adult who lives and identifies as a female even though they have been born as a different sex.

BIBLIOGRAPHY

Abrams, M. (2019). 64 terms that describe gender identity and expression. *Healthline*, December 20, https://www.healthline.com/health/different-genders

AHRC (Australian Human Rights Commission). 2019. *Guidelines for the Inclusion of Transgender and Gender Diverse People in Sport.* https://www.humanrights.gov.au/our-work/publications. https://www.sportaus.gov.au/__data/assets/pdf_file/0008/706184/Trans_and_Gender_Diverse_Guidelines_2019.pdf

Ainsworth, C. (2018). Sex redefined: the idea of 2 sexes is overly simplistic. *Scientific American -Nature Magazine,* October 22. https://www.scientificamerican.com/article/sex-redefined-the-idea-of-2-sexes-is-overly-simplistic1/

Allender, S., Cowburn, G., & Foster, C. (2006). Understanding participation in sport and physical activity among children and adults: a review of qualitative studies. *Health Education Research, 21* (6), 826–835. https://doi.org/10.1093/her/cyl063

Altimari, D. (2021). A Connecticut Court case has set off a flood of bills to limit transgender rights across the nation. *Hartford Courant*, April 25. https://www.courant.com/politics/hc-pol-pol-transgender-legislation-connecticut-20210425-ldg7jemdxzb2fmmlk2uvpuyskm-story.html.

Australian Government. *Sport Integrity Australia.* n.d. https://www.sportintegrity.gov.au.

American Psychiatric Association (2022). *Diagnostic and Statistical Manual of Mental Disorders*, *Revised 5th Edition* (DSM-5-TR). Arlington, VA, American Psychiatric Association

Bekker, S. (2022). *Holding Space*, Issue #15, 20 March 2022. Twitter @shereebekker.

Bermon, S., Garnier, P.Y., Hirschberg, A. L., Robinson, N., Giraud, S., Nicoli, R., Baume, N., Saugy, M., Fénichel, P., & Bruce, S. J. (2014). Serum androgen levels in elite female athletes. *Journal of Clinical Endocrinology and Metabolism, 99*(11), 4328-4335. https://doi.org/10.1210/jc.2014-1391.

Bianchi, A. (2017). Transgender women in sport." *Journal of the Philosophy of Sport, 44*(2), 229 -242. doi:10.1080/00948705.2017.1317602

Braumüller, B., Menzel, T., & Hartmann-Tews, I. (2020). Gender identities in organized sports - athletes' experiences and organizational strategies of inclusion. *Frontiers in Sociology*, 5. 17pp. https:// doi.org/10.3389/fsoc.2020.578213.

Cairney, J.; Veldhuizen, S., Kwan, M., Hay, J., & Faught, B. E. (2014). Biological age and sex-related declines in physical activity during adolescence, *Medicine and Science in Sports and Exercise, 46* (4), 730-735. PMID: 24056271. https://doi.org/10.1249/MSS.0000000000000168.

Coleman, D. L. (2017). Sex in sport. *Law and Contemporary Problems*, 80(63), 63–126. https://scholarship.law.duke.edu/lcp/vol80/iss4/5.

Coleman, D. L., Joyner, M. J. & Lopiano, D. (2020). Re-affirming the value of the sports exception to Title IX's general non-discrimination rule. *Duke Journal of Gender Law and Policy, 27*, 69-134. https://scholarship.law.duke.edu/djglp/vol27/iss1/

Collin, L.J., Reisner, S. L., Tangpricha, V., & Goodman, M. (2016). Prevalence of transgender depends on the 'case' definition: a systematic review. *The Journal of Sexual Medicine, 13*(4), 613-626. http://doi.org/10.1016/j.jsxm.2016.02.001.

Diaz, ES. & Bailey, J. M. (2023). Rapid onset gender dysphoria: parent report on 1655 possible cases. *Archives of Sexual Behavior, 52*, 1031-1043. https://doi.org/10.1007/s10508-023-02576-9. [Authors note: this paper was retracted by the publisher on 16 May 2023, due to 'lack of informed consent' from respondents to website ParentsofROGDKids.com. Other methodology, or statistics in the paper have not been called into question and the paper is still available on-line]

Deaner, R. O., Balish, S. M., & Lombardo, M. P. (2016). Sex differences in sports interests and motivation: an evolutionary perspective.

Evolutionary Behavioral Sciences, 10 (2), 73-97. https://doi.apa.org/doiLanding?doi=10.1037%2Febs0000049.

Devine, C. (2021). Female Olympians' voices: female sports categories and International Olympic Committee transgender guidelines. *International Review for the Sociology of Sport. 57*(3), 335-361. https://doi.org/10.1177/1012692211021559

Erikainen, S., Vincent, B.W., & Hopkins, A.L. (2022). Specific detriment: barriers and opportunities for non-binary inclusive sports in Scotland. *Journal of Sport & Social Issues, 46*(1),75 - 102. https://doi.org/10.1177/0193723520962937

FINA (2022). *FINA Inclusion Policy*, 24pp. https://resources.fina.org/fina/document/2022/06/19/525de003-51f4-47d3-8d5a-716dac5f77c7/FINA-INCLUSION-POLICY-AND-APPENDICES-FINAL-.pdf

Foddy, B. & Sevelescu, J. (2011) Time to re-evaluate gender segregation in athletics? *British Journal of Sports Medicine, 4,* 1184-1188. https://doi.org/10.1136/bjsm.2010.071639

Franke, W. W., & Berendonk, B. (1997). Hormonal doping and androgenization of athletes: a secret program of the German Democratic Republic government. *Clinical Chemistry, 43*(7), 1262-1279. https://doi.org/10.1093/clinchem/43.7.1262

Harter, S (2012) *The Construction of the Self: Developmental and Sociocultural Foundations*, (2nd ed.). Guilford Press. ISN 9781462522729.

Hilton, E.N. & Lundberg, T. R. (2021). Transgender women in the female category of sport: perspectives on testosterone suppression and performance advantage, *Sports Medicine, 51,* 199–214. https://doi.org/10.1007/s40279-020-01389-3

Goodman, M., Adams, N., Cornell, T., Kreukels, B., Motmans, J. & Coleman, E. (2019). Size and distribution of transgender and gender nonconforming populations: a narrative review. *Endocrinology and Metabolism Clinics of North America, 48*(2), 303–321. https://doi.org/10.1016/j.ecl.2019.01.001

Hämäläinen, M. (2014). A Sport with untapped potential to empower women. *Journal of the Philosophy of Sport, 41*(1), 53–63. https://doi.org/10.1080/00948705.2013.858637

Handelsman, D. J., Hirschberg, A. L. & Bermon, S. F. (2018). Circulating testosterone as the hormonal basis of sex differences in athletic performance. *Endocrine Review, 39*(5), 803–829. https://doi.org/10.1210/er.2018-00020

Harper, J., O'Donnell, E., Khorashad, B.S., McDermott, H., & Witcomb, G. (2021). How does hormone transition in transgender women change body composition, muscle strength and haemoglobin? Systematic review with a focus on implications for sport participation. *British Journal of Sports Medicine, 55*(15), 865–872. https://doi.org/10.1136/bjsports-2020-103106.

Harper, J., Martinez-Patino, M-J., Pigozzi, F. & Pitsiladis, Y. (2018). Implications of a third gender for elite sports. *Current Sports Medicine Reports, 17* (2), 42–44. https://doi.org/10.1249/JSR.0000000000000455

Herman, J.L., Flores, A.R., & O'Neill, K.K. (2022). How many adults and youth identify as transgender in the United States? *The Williams Institute*, UCLA School of Law. https://williamsinstitute.law.ucla.edu/wp-content/uploads/Trans-Pop-Update-Jun-2022.pdf

Hilton, E. N. & Lundberg, T. R. (2021). Transgender women in the female category of sport: perspectives on testosterone suppression and performance advantage. *Sports Medicine, 51*, 199–214. https://doi.org/10.1007/s40279-020-01389-3

International Athletics Federation (2018). *IAAF introduces new eligibility regulations for female classification.* https://worldathletics.org/news/press-release/eligibility-regulations-for-female-classifica

IOC (International Olympic Committee). (2015). *Consensus Meeting on Sex Reassignment and Hyperandrogenism, November 2015.* https://stillmed.olympic.org/Documents/Commissions_PDFfiles/Medical_commission/2015-11_ioc_consensus_meeting_on_sex_reassignment_and_hyperandrogenism-en.pdf

IOC (International Olympic Committee). (2021a). *IOC Framework on fairness, inclusion and non-discrimination on the basis of gender identity and sex variations.* Retrieved from https://olympics.com/ioc/documents/athletes/ioc-framework-on-fairness-inclusion-and-non-discrimination-on-the-basis-of-gender-identity-and-sex-variations

IOC (International Olympics Committee). (2021b). *Gender Equality and Inclusion Report 2021.* https://olympics.com/ioc/gender-equality

Ivy, V. (2021). If 'ifs' and 'buts' were candy and nuts: The failure of arguments against trans and intersex women's full and equal participation in women's sport. *Feminist Philosophy Quarterly, 7*(2), Article 3, 38pp. https://doi.org/10.5206/fpq/2021.2.10726

Kenny, D. (2020). Children and young people seeking and obtaining treatment for gender dysphoria in Australia: trends by state over time (2014 -2019): Update. Blog. 15 July. www.diannakenny.com.au/k-blog/item/15-children-and-young-people-seeking-and-obbtaining-tratmetn-for-gender-dysphoria-in-australia-trends-by-state-over-time-2014-2019-update

Knox, T., Anderson, L.C., & Heather, A. (2019). Transwomen in elite sport: scientific and ethical considerations. *Journal of Medical Ethics, 45*, 395-403. https://doi.org/10.1136/medethics-2018-105208

Magness, S. (2022). There's good reason for sports to be separated by sex. *The Atlantic,* 29 September. https://www.theatlantic.com/culture/archive/2022/09/sports-gender-sex-segregation-coed/671460/

Martinkova, I (2020). Unisex sports: challenging the binary. *Journal of Philosophy of Sport, 47*(2), 248-265. https://doi.org/10.1080/00948705.2020.1768861

Meyer, R. (2012). The 'golden ratio': The one number that describes how men's world records compare with women's. *The Atlantic*, 7 August. https://www.theatlantic.com/technology/archive/2012/08/the-golden-ratio-the-one-number-that-describes-how-mens-world-records-compare-with-womens/260758/

Nakrani, S. (2023). European court rules that Caster Semenya's human rights were violated. *The Guardian Australia Online*. https://www.theguardian.com/sport/2023/jul/11/caster-semenya-discriminated-against-by-testosterone-levels-rules-echr.

Pakaslahti, A. (2017). Compensated sex-integrated individual competitions in ski jumping: a response to Hamalainen. *Sport, Ethics and Philosophy, 11*(2), 219–223. https://doi.org/10.1080/17511321.2016.1272130

Parker, H.E., Hands, B., & Rose, E. (2021). Australian transgender guidelines for sport, Part 1: Biological perspectives, fairness, and physical safety in women's sport. *The International Journal of Sport and Society, 13*(1), 23-38. https://doi.org/10.18848/2152-7857/CGP/v13i01/23-38

Parker, H., Hands, B., & Rose, E. (2021). Australian transgender guidelines for sport, Part 2: Implications for female competition integrity, *The International Journal of Sport and Society, 13*(1), 55-70. https://doi.org/10.18848/2152-7857/CGP/v13i01/55-70.

Pigozzi, F., Bigard, X., Steinacker, J., et al. 2022. Joint position statement of The International Federation of Sports Medicine (FIMS) and European Federation of Sports Medicine Associations (EFSMA on The IOC Framework on Fairness, Inclusion and Non-Discrimination Based on Gender Identity and Sex Variations. *British Medical Journal, Open Sport & Exercise Medicine, 8*, e001273. https://doi.org/10.1136/bmjsem-2021-001273

Pike, J. (2021). Safety, fairness, and inclusion: transgender athletes and the essence of rugby. *Journal of the Philosophy of Sport, 48* (2),155-168, https://doi.org/10.1080/00948705.2020.1863814.

Pike, J., Hilton, E., & Howe, L.A. (2021). *Fair game: Biology, fairness and transgender athletes in women's sport*. Macdonald-Laurier Institute. https://macdonaldlaurier.ca/files/pdf/Dec2021_Fair_game_Pike_Hilton_Howe_PAPER_FWeb.pdf.

Schultz, J. (2019). Good enough? The 'wicked' use of testosterone for defining femaleness in women's sport. Sport in Society, 24(4), 607-627. https://doi.org/10.1080/17430437.2019.1703684

Semenya, Caster (Wikipedia). https://en.wikipedia.org/wiki/Caster_Semenya

Sharma, D. (2018). Deciphering the role of the Barr Body in malignancy. *Sultan Qaboos University Medical Journal.* 17 (4), 389–397. https://doi.org/10.18295%2Fsqumj.2017.17.04.003

Sailors, P. R. (2014). Mixed competition and mixed messages. *Journal of the Philosophy of Sport, 41*(1), 65–77. https://doi.org/10.1080/00948705-2013-858398

Sailors, P. R. (2016). Off the beaten path: Should women compete against men? *Sport in Society, 19*(8–9), 1125–1137. https://doi.org/10.1080/17430437.2015.1096255

Sailors, P.R. (2020). Transgender and intersex athletes and the women's category in sport. *Sport, Ethics and Philosophy, 14*(4): 419–431. https://doi.org/10.1080/17511321.2020.1756904

Sallis, J. F. (1993) Epidemiology of physical activity and fitness in children and adolescents. *Critical Reviews of Food Science and Nutrition. 33*(4-5), 405–408. https://doi.org/10.1080/10408399309527639

Save Women's Sport (nd). *Males in female sports* https://savewomenssports.com/males-in-female-sports-1

Scanlon, P (2023). *"You Will Regret It!" NCAA Swimmer Breaks Her Silence*. https://www.youtube.com/watch?v=p3L-oY5l_so.

Scanlon, P. (2023). *Former teammate of Lia Thomas unveils herself.* An interview with Matt Walsh, The Daily Wire. https://www.youtube.com/watch?v=sRUjW3Vvyws.

Sharrow, E. A. (2021). Sports, transgender rights and the body politics of cisgender supremacy. *Laws, 10*(3), 63 https://doi.org/10.3390/laws10030063.

Sissons, C. (2021). Typical testosterone levels in males and females. *Medical News Today* (updated January 6, 2023) https://www.medicalnewstoday.com/articles/323085#typical-levels

Soares, J., Antuennes, H., & Van Den Tillaar, R. (2013). A comparison between boys and girls about the motives for the participation in school sport. *Journal of Physical Education and Sport 13*(3), 303-307. http://dx.doi.org/10.7752/jpes.2013.03050

Sonksen, P. H., Holt, R. I. G., Bohning, W., Guha, N., Cowan D. A., Bartlett, C., & Bohning, D. (2018). Why do endocrine profiles in elite athletes differ between sports? *Clinical Diabetes and Endocrinology, 4*(3). https://doi.org/10.1186/s40842-017-0050-3

Spizzirri, G., Eufrásio, R., Lima, M.C.P., de Carvelho Nunes, H. R., Kreukels, B. P. C., Steensma, T. D., & Addo, C. H. N. Proportion of people identified as transgender and non-binary gender in Brazil. *Scientific Reports, 11*, 2240. https://doi.org/10.1038/s41598-021-81411-4

Thomas, Jerry R. and K E French. (1985). Gender differences across age in motor performance: A meta-analysis. *Psychological Bulletin, 98*(2), 260-282. PMID: 3901062

Tucker, R. (2019). On transgender athletes and performance advantages. *The Science of Sport Blog*, 24 March. https://sportsscientists.com/2019/03/on-transgender-athletes-and-performance-advantages/

Tucker, R. (2021). https://twitter.com/Scienceofsport/status/1460688851408760833.

Ulrich, D. A. (2013). *Test of Gross Motor Development* (Third edition). Austin, TX: Pro Ed Inc.

UK Sports Councils. (2021). *New guidance for transgender inclusion in domestic sport. Sport England,* September 30, 2021. https://www.sportengland.org/news/new-guidance-transgender-inclusion-domestic-sport-published.

Wizeman, T. M., & Pardue, M. L. 2001. *Exploring the Biological Contributions to Human Health: Does Sex Matter?* Washington DC: National Academies Press. https://www.ncbi.nlm.nih.gov/books/NBK222291/#ddd00049

Wiik, A., Lundberg, T.R., Rullman, E., Andersson, D.P., Holmberg, M., Mandić, M., Brismar, T.B. et al. 2020. Muscle strength, size, and composition following 12 months of gender-affirming treatment in transgender individuals. *Journal of Clinical Endocrinology Metabolism, 105*(3), e805–e813. https://doi.org:10.1210/clinem/dgz247.

Worley, K. (2014). Gender struggles for women to find equality in sport: when the ioc has gone too far to determine a woman's eligibility to compete. *6th IWG World Conference on Women and Sport, Helsinki, Catalyst eNewsletter.* August. https://web.archive.org/web/20181002162605/https://iwg--gti-org.directo.fi/catalyst/august-2014/gender-struggles-for-women-to-fi/#Gender%20struggles%20for%20women%20to%20find%20equality%20in%20sport

World Athletics. (2019). *World Athletics Eligibility Regulations for Transgender Athletes.* Monaco: World Athletics. https://www.worldathletics.org

World Rugby. (2020). *Transgender Guideline, Effective 9 October 2020.* Dublin: World Rugby House. https://www.world.rugby/the-game/player-welfare/guidelines/transgender

Zucker, K. J. (2017). Epidemiology of gender dysphoria and transgender identity. *Sexual Health, 14*(5): 404–411. https://doi.org/10.1071/SH17067.

www.ingramcontent.com/pod-product-compliance
Lightning Source LLC
Chambersburg PA
CBHW072045160426
43197CB00014B/2629